P.E. Curriculum Guide

by
Mel J. Nicks, M.A.
Professor Emeritus
St. Norbert College
DePere, Wisconsin

John Ortwerth
Chairman, Physical Education Department
Quincy College
Quincy, Illinois

illustrated by Kevin Nobis

D1104061

Cover by Dan Grossmann

Copyright © Good Apple, Inc., 1984

ISBN No. 0-86653-262-5

Good Apple
A Division of Frank Schaffer Publications, Inc.
23740 Hawthorne Boulevard
Torrance, CA 90505-5927

ACKNOWLEDGEMENTS

St. Norbert College Elementary Preparatory Classes
Green Bay Diocesan Curriculum Committee
Illustrator, Kevin Nobis
Green Bay Diocesan Parochial School Teachers' Pilot Program
President's Council for Physical Fitness—Test Manual

THE WHITE HOUSE
Washington

August 1965

On behalf of the President I wish to congratulate the Catholic Diocese of Green Bay, Wisconsin, on publishing this important elementary curriculum handbook for physical education. While most people recognize that exercise and sports have immediate value, far too few recognize these activities as doing anything substantial to prepare pupils for life beyond their school years.

There are three pressing reasons why a good physical education program is essential today. First, our way of life no longer provides the vigorous physical activities necessary to help physical development. Second, recent research indicates a direct relationship between physical fitness and academic and social performance, and third, the increase in leisure time makes it necessary to prepare our people to enjoy and use it constructively.

I am sure this curriculum handbook will be an excellent vehicle and we wish you success in your school programs.

Stan Musial
Consultant to the President
on Physical Fitness

PREFACE

This revision of the 1965 Curriculum Manual for Elementary Physical Education was developed to upgrade the material, facilitate the use of the manual, and add sections which will improve programs of physical education in grades 1, 2, 3, 4, 5, 6. Classroom teachers responsible for the teaching of physical education have been enthusiastic about its use in various sections of the country, in both private and public schools, and have urged the authors to undertake this task.

The original manual was an outgrowth of years of teaching elementary physical education curriculum courses at St. Norbert College. The co-author, John G. Ortwerth, has added his expertise. The manual was first published to provide a comprehensively sound program for the Diocese of Green Bay which would be basically coeducational, and the pilot program proved it to be practical and workable.

The purposes are as follows:
1. A curriculum that can be administered by the classroom teacher who has not had specialized training in physical education
2. A day-by-day, weekly, monthly, yearly curriculum for grades 1, 2, 3, 4, 5, 6
3. A well-balanced curriculum that is graded to maturation levels
4. A curriculum that can be carried out in minimum space facilities, with minimum equipment and a limited budget

TABLE OF CONTENTS

PROCEDURE

I. General

The curriculum schedules can be adjusted to provide for various time allotments for physical education and number of periods per week. Each day's activities are based on a thirty-minute time interval. If one class per week is assigned, use those activities listed under session number one; if two periods, those marked sessions one and two; etc., for three, four, or five periods per week.

II. Daily Class

1. Start class with 3-5 minutes of the warm-up activity listed in the day's curriculum.
2. Group class and introduce activity.
3. Guide class throughout activity.

III. Explanation of the DAILY SQUARE

W-A
Movement
8-7

W—Warm-up
A—See page xvi
Movement—Section
8-7—Activities for the day

OBJECTIVES OF PHYSICAL EDUCATION

1. To promote physical growth, development and maintenance through activities that develop strength, vigor, vitality, skill and coordination.

2. To contribute to the development of social competencies in relationships with others.

3. To enjoy and participate in wholesome physical recreation throughout life.

4. To develop useful skills in physical activities.

CURRICULUM

PERCENTAGE GRAPH OF PROGRAMS FOR GRADES ONE, TWO, AND THREE

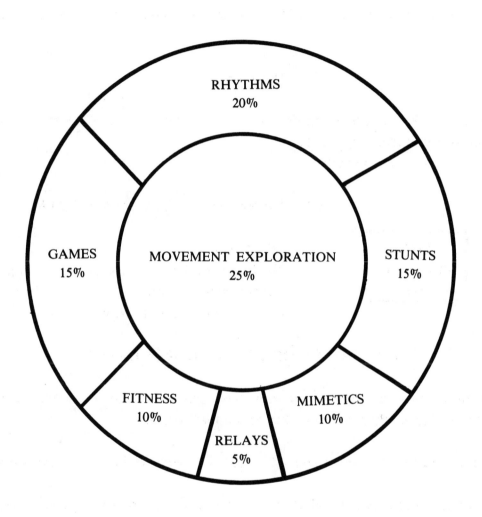

GRADE 1 — QUARTER 1

Week	Session 1	Session 2	Session 3	Session 4	Session 5
1	* W-A MOVEMENT 8-7	W-B STUNTS 349-347	W-C RHYTHMS 221	W-D MIMETICS Page 48	W-E MOVEMENT 9-10
2	W-F FITNESS 361-332	W-A RHYTHMS 221	W-B GAMES 75-179	W-C MOVEMENT 10	W-D RELAY 453
3	W-E RHYTHMS 221	W-F STUNTS 310-406-322	W-A MOVEMENT 21-22	W-B GAMES 102-366-279	W-C FITNESS 366-279
4	W-D STUNTS 239-323	W-E MOVEMENT 9-22	W-F MIMETICS Page 48	W-A RELAY 432-437	W-B RHYTHMS 242
5	W-C GAMES 161-133	W-D FITNESS 330-412	W-E MOVEMENT 8-23	W-F RHYTHMS 202	W-A MOVEMENT 9-10-22
6	W-B GAMES 78-179	W-C STUNTS 282-315	W-D RHYTHMS 257	W-E MOVEMENT 21	W-F MIMETICS Page 48
7	W-A RELAY 418-431	W-B MOVEMENT 56-57	W-C STUNTS 239-390	W-D FITNESS 350-366	W-E RHYTHMS 200
8	W-F GAMES 176	W-A RHYTHMS 209	W-B MOVEMENT 1-2	W-C STUNTS 299-372	W-D MOVEMENT 23-1
9	W-E MOVEMENT 23-2	W-F RHYTHMS Choice	W-A FITNESS 410-408	W-B GAMES 189	W-C MIMETICS Page 48

*W = Warm-up

GRADE 1 — QUARTER 2

Week	Session 1	Session 2	Session 3	Session 4	Session 5
1	* W-A MOVEMENT 1-9	W-B RHYTHMS 219	W-C GAMES 175	W-D MIMETICS Page 48	W-E STUNTS 309-333-372
2	W-F STUNTS 239-390	W-A RELAY 421-443	W-B MOVEMENT 23-3	W-C MOVEMENT 21-22	W-D RHYTHMS 240
3	W-E GAMES 131-1	W-F FITNESS 1	W-A MIMETICS Page 48	W-B MOVEMENT 1-2	W-C RHYTHMS 240
4	W-D STUNTS 295-350	W-E RHYTHMS 257	W-F GAMES 85	W-A FITNESS 24	W-B MOVEMENT 3-8
5	W-C GAMES 116	W-D MIMETICS Page 48	W-E STUNTS Choice	W-F MOVEMENT 2-21	W-A RHYTHMS 238
6	W-B STUNTS 376-389	W-C RELAY 423-432	W-D FITNESS 289-298	W-E MOVEMENT 1-11	W-F RHYTHMS 238
7	W-A MIMETICS Page 48	W-B RHYTHMS 202-221	W-C MOVEMENT 36-43	W-D GAMES 82	W-E MOVEMENT 2-9
8	W-F MOVEMENT 1-2-9-21	W-A GAMES 111-188	W-B RHYTHMS 270	W-C STUNTS 282-284	W-D FITNESS 367-346
9	W-E GAMES 151	W-F RHYTHMS 270	W-A MIMETICS Page 48	W-B MOVEMENT 23-3	W-C STUNTS 346

*W = Warm-up

GRADE 1 — QUARTER 3

Week	Session 1	Session 2	Session 3	Session 4	Session 5
1	* W-A MOVEMENT 10-23	W-B RHYTHMS 246	W-C GAMES 72	W-D STUNTS 284-350	W-E MIMETICS Page 48
2	W-F STUNTS 381-321	W-A MOVEMENT 21-22	W-B RELAY 427-440	W-C RHYTHMS 221	W-D MOVEMENT 12
3	W-E GAMES 79	W-F MIMETICS Page 48	W-A FITNESS 12	W-B MOVEMENT 3-24	W-C RHYTHMS 254
4	W-D MOVEMENT 1-11	W-E FITNESS 412-348-361-366	W-F GAMES 88	W-A STUNTS 281-295	W-B RHYTHMS 221
5	W-C GAMES 97-192	W-D RHYTHMS 268	W-E STUNTS 381	W-F MOVEMENT 12-24	W-A RHYTHMS 243
6	W-B STUNTS 317-349	W-C RELAY 424-417	W-D MOVEMENT 24-25	W-E RHYTHMS Page 47	W-F FITNESS 457-426
7	W-A RHYTHMS 264	W-B MIMETICS Page 48	W-C MOVEMENT 2-12	W-D GAMES 99	W-E MOVEMENT 25-36
8	W-F MOVEMENT 3-24	W-A GAMES 100-174	W-B STUNTS 321	W-C RHYTHMS 270	W-D FITNESS 303-322
9	W-E GAMES 180	W-F RHYTHMS 232	W-A STUNTS 308-358	W-B MOVEMENT 36-37	W-C MIMETICS Page 48

*W = Warm-up

GRADE 1 — QUARTER 4

Week	Session 1	Session 2	Session 3	Session 4	Session 5
1	* W-A MOVEMENT 11-36	W-B GAMES 176-158	W-C RHYTHMS 229	W-D STUNTS 327-356	W-E MIMETICS Page 48
2	W-F RHYTHMS 239	W-A STUNTS 357-352	W-B RELAY 428-433	W-C FITNESS 368-374	W-D MOVEMENT 12-25
3	W-E GAMES 104	W-F MOVEMENT 42	W-A RHYTHMS 214	W-B MIMETICS Page 48	W-C MOVEMENT 24-37
4	W-D FITNESS 412-348-361-366	W-E GAMES 75-101	W-F MOVEMENT 43	W-A RHYTHMS Page 47	W-B STUNTS 239
5	W-C MIMETICS Page 48	W-D GAMES 181	W-E STUNTS 390-302	W-F MOVEMENT 37-43	W-A RHYTHMS 202-239
6	W-B RELAY 416-414	W-C FITNESS 412-348-361-366	W-D RHYTHMS 214	W-E MOVEMENT 12-42	W-F STUNTS 296-314
7	W-A GAMES 129-149	W-B MIMETICS Choice Page 48	W-C RHYTHMS 208	W-D MOVEMENT 24-43	W-E FITNESS 429
8	W-F MOVEMENT 25-42	W-A GAMES Choice	W-B RHYTHMS 208	W-C MOVEMENT Review	W-D STUNTS Choice
9	W-E STUNTS Choice	W-F MIMETICS Choice Page 48	W-A GAMES Choice	W-B RHYTHMS Review	W-C FITNESS 429

*W = Warm-up

viii

GRADE 2 — QUARTER 1

Week	Session 1	Session 2	Session 3	Session 4	Session 5
1	* W-A MOVEMENT 8-9	W-B GAMES 71-116	W-C RHYTHMS 208	W-D STUNTS 282-347-349	W-E MIMETICS Page 48
2	W-F RHYTHMS 243	W-A FITNESS 361-366	W-B MOVEMENT 10-21	W-C RELAY 435-434	W-D MOVEMENT 22-23
3	W-E STUNTS 372-384-309	W-F MIMETICS Page 48	W-A GAMES 149-147	W-B RHYTHMS 214	W-C MOVEMENT 9-10-21
4	W-D GAMES 95-86	W-E MOVEMENT 3-11	W-F FITNESS 412-21	W-A RHYTHMS 243	W-B MOVEMENT 1-2
5	W-C MOVEMENT 12-24	W-D FITNESS 361-457	W-E RELAY 417-422	W-F STUNTS 307-382	W-A RHYTHMS 216
6	W-B RHYTHMS 240	W-C STUNTS 350-281-305	W-D MIMETICS Page 48	W-E GAMES 169-158	W-F MOVEMENT 25-36
7	W-A FITNESS 67	W-B MOVEMENT 37-42	W-C STUNTS 317-352-358	W-D MOVEMENT 22-23-1	W-E RHYTHMS 254
8	W-F GAMES 132-165	W-A RELAY 437-418	W-B FITNESS 361-427	W-C RHYTHMS 202-239	W-D MOVEMENT 2-3-11
9	W-E MOVEMENT 2-8-10	W-F GAMES 179-133	W-A MIMETICS Football Page 48	W-B STUNTS 318-345-257	W-C RHYTHMS 216

*W = Warm-up

GRADE 2 — QUARTER 2

Week	Session 1	Session 2	Session 3	Session 4	Session 5
1	* W-A MOVEMENT 43-44	W-B GAMES 99-97	W-C RHYTHMS 232	W-D STUNTS 413-307-382	W-E MIMETICS Page 48
2	W-F FITNESS 361-366	W-A RELAY 421-426	W-B STUNTS 318-345	W-C MOVEMENT 24-36	W-D RHYTHMS 223
3	W-E STUNTS 352-384	W-F RHYTHMS 216	W-A FITNESS 412-361 348-366	W-B MOVEMENT 25-42	W-C MIMETICS Page 48
4	W-D MOVEMENT 36-37	W-E GAMES 105-79	W-F MOVEMENT 33-44	W-A RHYTHMS 261	W-B GAMES 169-75
5	W-C RHYTHMS 257	W-D MIMETICS Page 48	W-E STUNTS 294-375	W-F FITNESS 412-361 348-366	W-A MOVEMENT 42-44
6	W-B RELAY 421-437-436	W-C MOVEMENT 33-43	W-D GAMES 147-176	W-E MIMETICS Page 48	W-F RHYTHMS 233
7	W-A RHYTHMS 229	W-B STUNTS 358-384	W-C MOVEMENT 33-34	W-D FITNESS 67	W-E MOVEMENT 24-42
8	W-F GAMES 124-82	W-A MOVEMENT 34-35	W-B MIMETICS Page 48	W-C STUNTS 327-365-356	W-D RHYTHMS 223
9	W-E GAMES 132-180	W-F STUNTS Choice	W-A RHYTHMS 261	W-B GAMES 71-174	W-C MOVEMENT 34-44

*W = Warm-up

GRADE 2 — QUARTER 3

Week	Session 1	Session 2	Session 3	Session 4	Session 5
1	* W-A FITNESS 348-361 366-412	W-B GAMES 136-185	W-C MOVEMENT 37-33	W-D RHYTHMS 262	W-E STUNTS 281-340
2	W-F GAMES 108	W-A STUNTS 295-305-350	W-B MOVEMENT 2-5-3	W-C MIMETICS Page 48	W-D MOVEMENT 35-69
3	W-E STUNTS 284-287-372	W-F RHYTHMS 264	W-A MOVEMENT 43-33	W-B FITNESS 279-283	W-C RHYTHMS 217-257
4	W-D RELAY 416-423	W-E GAMES 182-82	W-F MIMETICS Page 48	W-A RHYTHMS 198	W-B MOVEMENT 35-44
5	W-C RHYTHMS 202-257	W-D RELAY 438-439	W-E STUNTS 315-335	W-F GAMES 122	W-A MOVEMENT 69-70
6	W-B MOVEMENT 34-69	W-C GAMES 108	W-D MIMETICS Page 48	W-E MOVEMENT 44-33	W-F STUNTS 340-341
7	W-A RHYTHMS 199	W-B FITNESS 14-22	W-C STUNTS 345-384	W-D RHYTHMS 233	W-E MOVEMENT 5-70
8	W-F MOVEMENT 35-70	W-A MIMETICS Page 48	W-B GAMES 145	W-C FITNESS 67	W-D RHYTHMS 262
9	W-E GAMES 122	W-F STUNTS 369-381-257	W-A RHYTHMS 198	W-B MOVEMENT 69-5	W-C MIMETICS Page 48

*W = Warm-up

GRADE 2 — QUARTER 4

Week	Session 1	Session 2	Session 3	Session 4	Session 5
1	* W-A GAMES 167	W-B MOVEMENT 35-69	W-C RHYTHMS 231	W-D STUNTS 378-380	W-E MOVEMENT 5-6
2	W-F FITNESS 348-361 366-412	W-A STUNTS 307-278-318	W-B MOVEMENT 9-21	W-C GAMES 153-181	W-D RHYTHMS 200
3	W-E STUNTS 373-378-345	W-F MIMETICS Page 48	W-A RELAY 417-419	W-B RHYTHMS 201	W-C MOVEMENT 10-22
4	W-D MIMETICS Page 48	W-E GAMES 178	W-F FITNESS 348-361-366-412	W-A MOVEMENT 6-7	W-B RHYTHMS 255
5	W-C RHYTHMS 201-202	W-D FITNESS 37	W-E MOVEMENT 1-2	W-F GAMES 156	W-A MOVEMENT 3-23
6	W-B GAMES 167	W-C STUNTS 378-371	W-D FITNESS 429	W-E RHYTHMS 199	W-F MOVEMENT 7-18
7	W-A RELAY 416-421	W-B RHYTHMS 204	W-C MIMETICS Page 48	W-D MOVEMENT 11-12	W-E STUNTS 335-332
8	W-F MOVEMENT 18-19	W-A STUNTS 371-375	W-B FITNESS 348-361 366-412	W-C GAMES 177	W-D RHYTHMS 231
9	W-E MOVEMENT 7-19	W-F RHYTHMS Choice	W-A MIMETICS Page 48	W-B GAMES 178	W-C STUNTS Choice

*W = Warm-up

GRADE 3 — QUARTER 1

Week	Session 1	Session 2	Session 3	Session 4	Session 5
1	* W-A FITNESS 67	W-B GAMES 176-130	W-C MOVEMENT 8-52 21-24	W-D RHYTHMS 243	W-E MOVEMENT 9-10-23
2	W-F STUNTS 280-305	W-A RHYTHMS 251	W-B FITNESS 348-361 366-412	W-C MOVEMENT 1-2	W-D MIMETICS Page 48
3	W-E GAMES 153-75	W-F RELAY 417-436	W-A STUNTS 330-412-369	W-B MOVEMENT 3-11	W-C RHYTHMS 216
4	W-D RHYTHMS 251-209	W-E MOVEMENT 12-24	W-F RELAY 419-425	W-A FITNESS 361-366 348-412	W-B GAMES 121-93
5	W-C GAMES 108	W-D FITNESS 348-303-311	W-E MOVEMENT 25-36	W-F RHYTHMS 275	W-A MOVEMENT 37-42
6	W-B RELAY 416-442	W-C MIMETICS Page 48	W-D RHYTHMS 223-257	W-E MOVEMENT 43-44	W-F STUNTS 296-390-327
7	W-A RHYTHMS 275-250	W-B STUNTS 257-378	W-C GAMES 109	W-D MIMETICS Page 48	W-E MOVEMENT 33-34
8	W-F MOVEMENT 35-69	W-A FITNESS 366-325-329	W-B STUNTS 305-280-339	W-C RHYTHMS 269	W-D MIMETICS Page 48
9	W-E MOVEMENT 6-7	W-F GAMES 121-113	W-A STUNTS 342-305	W-B MOVEMENT 5-70	W-C RHYTHMS 261

*W = Warm-up

GRADE 3 — QUARTER 2

Week	Session 1	Session 2	Session 3	Session 4	Session 5
1	* W-A GAMES 157-114	W-B MOVEMENT 25-42	W-C STUNTS 305-308-307	W-D RHYTHMS 269-220	W-E MOVEMENT 7-18
2	W-F FITNESS 429	W-A RHYTHMS 234	W-B GAMES 115	W-C MOVEMENT 8-21-24	W-D STUNTS 413-296-320
3	W-E STUNTS 335-341-345	W-F MIMETICS Page 48	W-A MOVEMENT 34-35	W-B GAMES 106-130	W-C RHYTHMS 236-239
4	W-D RELAY 418-441	W-E GAMES 75-90	W-F FITNESS 329-328-311	W-A RHYTHMS 234	W-B MOVEMENT 18-19
5	W-C RHYTHMS 206	W-D STUNTS 376-365-364	W-E MOVEMENT 19-70	W-F RELAY 421-437	W-A MOVEMENT 7-69
6	W-B GAMES 93-114	W-C MOVEMENT 33-69	W-D STUNTS 375-355	W-E RHYTHMS 262-202	W-F MIMETICS Page 48
7	W-A RHYTHMS 206-256	W-B FITNESS 307-430	W-C GAMES 164	W-D MOVEMENT 19-20	W-E MIMETICS Page 48
8	W-F MIMETICS Page 48	W-A MOVEMENT 7-18	W-B STUNTS 321-390-314	W-C FITNESS 348-361 366-412	W-D RHYTHMS 252
9	W-E MOVEMENT 6-20	W-F STUNTS 292-386	W-A GAMES 115	W-B MIMETICS Page 48	W-C RHYTHMS 198-257

*W = Warm-up

GRADE 3 — QUARTER 3

Week	Session 1	Session 2	Session 3	Session 4	Session 5
1	* W-A RHYTHMS 252-209	W-B FITNESS 336-334	W-C STUNTS 371-306	W-D MOVEMENT 33-44	W-E MOVEMENT 20-26
2	W-F GAMES 71-85	W-A STUNTS 290-308-305	W-B MIMETICS Page 48	W-C MOVEMENT 19-20	W-D RHYTHMS 203
3	W-E MOVEMENT 44-26	W-F RHYTHMS 199-202	W-A GAMES 183	W-B RELAY 432-434	W-C STUNTS 318-355-357
4	W-D FITNESS 9	W-E MIMETICS Page 48	W-F RHYTHMS 203-250	W-A MOVEMENT 26-27	W-B GAMES 83-82
5	W-C RELAY 422-426	W-D MOVEMENT 5-18	W-E STUNTS 413-239	W-F RHYTHMS 212	W-A MOVEMENT 6-7
6	W-B MIMETICS Page 48	W-C RHYTHMS 231-239	W-D GAMES 83-116	W-E STUNTS 292-278-386	W-F MOVEMENT 36-26
7	W-A GAMES 185-182	W-B STUNTS Choice	W-C RHYTHMS 212	W-D FITNESS 377-370-374	W-E MOVEMENT 27-28
8	W-F MOVEMENT 69-70	W-A GAMES 139-125	W-B MIMETICS Page 48	W-C FITNESS 301-30	W-D RHYTHMS 227
9	W-E STUNTS 379-279	W-F MOVEMENT 26-28	W-A GAMES 120	W-B RHYTHMS 255	W-C MIMETICS Page 48

*W = Warm-up

GRADE 3 — QUARTER 4

Week	Session 1	Session 2	Session 3	Session 4	Session 5
1	* W-A GAMES 517	W-B RHYTHMS 227-219	W-C MOVEMENT 42-43	W-D STUNTS 334-335	W-E MOVEMENT 28-67
2	W-F STUNTS 296-314-257	W-A MOVEMENT 12-25	W-B GAMES 168-183	W-C RHYTHMS 226	W-D MIMETICS Page 48
3	W-E FITNESS 348-361 366-412	W-F STUNTS 279-287-289	W-A MOVEMENT 27-28	W-B GAMES 187-186	W-C RHYTHMS 204
4	W-D GAMES 112-169	W-E RELAY 435-441	W-F MOVEMENT 67-68	W-A RHYTHMS 226-256	W-B FITNESS 141-430
5	W-C RHYTHMS 213	W-D STUNTS 286-404-407	W-E MOVEMENT 27-68	W-F FITNESS 50	W-A MOVEMENT 19-20
6	W-B MIMETICS Page 48	W-C MOVEMENT 37-42-70	W-D GAMES 80-179	W-E STUNTS 342-341	W-F RHYTHMS Choice
7	W-A RELAY 434-450	W-B RHYTHMS 213-209	W-C MOVEMENT 68	W-D GAMES 512-510	W-E MIMETICS Page 48
8	W-F MOVEMENT 67-68	W-A GAMES Choice	W-B STUNTS 334-289	W-C RHYTHMS Choice	W-D FITNESS 289-290-414
9	W-E MOVEMENT Choice	W-F STUNTS Choice	W-A FITNESS 348-361 366-412	W-B MIMETICS Page 48	W-C RHYTHMS Choice

*W = Warm-up

PERCENTAGE GRAPH OF PROGRAMS FOR GRADES FOUR, FIVE, SIX

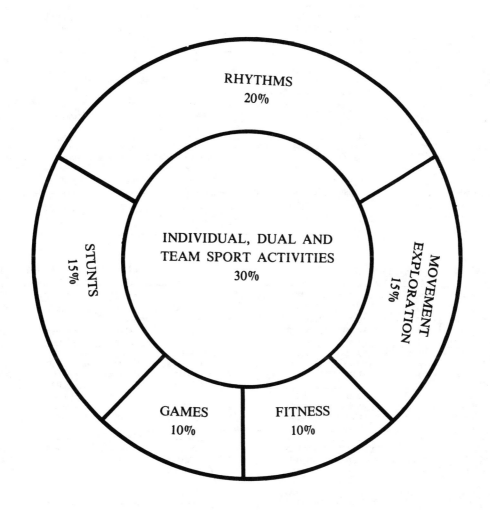

GRADE 4 — QUARTER 1

Week	Session 1	Session 2	Session 3	Session 4	Session 5
1	* W-A FITNESS 348-361-366-412	W-B LEAD-UPS Page 118	W-C RHYTHMS 222	W-D MOVEMENT 29-30	W-E GAMES 92
2	W-F STUNTS 305-280-336	W-A MOVEMENT 31-50	W-B LEAD-UPS Page 119	W-C RHYTHMS 221	W-D FITNESS 14-361
3	W-E STUNTS 316-368	W-F RHYTHMS 261	W-A LEAD-UPS Page 118	W-B MOVEMENT 32-51	W-C GAMES 94
4	W-D RHYTHMS 267-224	W-E LEAD-UPS 509 Page 118	W-F STUNTS Page 71	W-A FITNESS 296-291	W-B LEAD-UPS Page 119
5	W-C MOVEMENT 52-53	W-D GAMES 126	W-E LEAD-UPS 140 Page 118	W-F LEAD-UPS 140 Page 119	W-A STUNTS Page 71
6	W-B LEAD-UPS 148	W-C FITNESS 348-361-366-412	W-D RHYTHMS 237	W-E LEAD-UPS 107	W-F MOVEMENT 46-64
7	W-A RHYTHMS 212	W-B MOVEMENT 40-63	W-C GAMES 117	W-D LEAD-UPS 109	W-E LEAD-UPS 148
8	W-F MOVEMENT 41-47	W-A LEAD-UPS 107	W-B LEAD-UPS 148	W-C RHYTHMS 261	W-D STUNTS 373-359-360
9	W-E LEAD-UPS 137-119	W-F RHYTHMS 267-237	W-A STUNTS 374-287-301	W-B FITNESS 22-23	W-C GAMES 159

*W = Warm-up

GRADE 4 — QUARTER 2

Week	Session 1	Session 2	Session 3	Session 4	Session 5
1	* W-A FITNESS 348-361-366-412	W-B LEAD-UPS 107	W-C GAMES 117	W-D STUNTS 280-305-277	W-E GAMES 150
2	W-F LEAD-UPS 148	W-A RHYTHMS 253	W-B FITNESS 13	W-C RHYTHMS 271	W-D GAMES 126
3	W-E MOVEMENT 36	W-F MOVEMENT 29	W-A LEAD-UPS 119	W-B RHYTHMS 222-224	W-C LEAD-UPS Page 115
4	W-D LEAD-UPS Page 116	W-E FITNESS 348-361-366-412	W-F STUNTS 316-338-336	W-A RHYTHMS 267	W-B RHYTHMS 237
5	W-C GAMES 135	W-D LEAD-UPS Pages 116, 117	W-E LEAD-UPS 476 Page 117	W-F MOVEMENT 51	W-A MOVEMENT 52
6	W-B STUNTS 379-380-374	W-C STUNTS 368-328-329	W-D FITNESS 348-361-366-412	W-E LEAD-UPS 98	W-F MOVEMENT 51
7	W-A LEAD-UPS 509	W-B RHYTHMS 249	W-C GAMES 150	W-D STUNTS 287-374-375	W-E RHYTHMS 253
8	W-F RHYTHMS 249	W-A LEAD-UPS 476 Page 117	W-B STUNTS 287-359-368	W-C MOVEMENT 38	W-D LEAD-UPS 509
9	W-E STUNTS 337-360-361	W-F MOVEMENT 39	W-A LEAD-UPS 173	W-B RHYTHMS 245	W-C LEAD-UPS 513

*W = Warm-up

GRADE 4 — QUARTER 3

Week	Session 1	Session 2	Session 3	Session 4	Session 5
1	* W-A MOVEMENT 29-31	W-B LEAD-UPS 157	W-C RHYTHMS 273-224	W-D FITNESS 348-361-366-412	W-E LEAD-UPS Page 120
2	W-F GAMES 150	W-A STUNTS 322-316-338	W-B RHYTHMS 212	W-C MOVEMENT 38-63	W-D LEAD-UPS 91
3	W-E STUNTS 336-360-348	W-F RHYTHMS 222-247	W-A LEAD-UPS 515	W-B MOVEMENT 50-61	W-C RHYTHMS 249-267
4	W-D LEAD-UPS Page 120	W-E GAMES 152	W-F STUNTS 434-406	W-A LEAD-UPS 157	W-B FITNESS 348-361-366-412
5	W-C LEAD-UPS Page 115	W-D MOVEMENT 46-48	W-E RHYTHMS 252	W-F STUNTS 373-285-284	W-E RHYTHMS 237
6	W-F RHYTHMS 245	W-A GAMES 170	W-B MOVEMENT 48-58	W-C LEAD-UPS Page 115	W-D LEAD-UPS Page 120
7	W-E LEAD-UPS 511	W-F STUNTS 287-324-359	W-A LEAD-UPS 511	W-B RHYTHMS 273	W-C MOVEMENT 53-41
8	W-D MOVEMENT 55-65	W-E FITNESS 84-23	W-F GAMES 117	W-A LEAD-UPS 91	W-B STUNTS 296-390-320
9	W-C RHYTHMS 253	W-D LEAD-UPS 511-515	W-E FITNESS 291-296-346	W-F STUNTS 313-311	W-A LEAD-UPS 141

*W = Warm-up

GRADE 4 — QUARTER 4

Week	Session 1	Session 2	Session 3	Session 4	Session 5
1	* W-A GAMES 170	W-B MOVEMENT 29-30	W-C FITNESS 348-361-366-412	W-D RHYTHMS 253-249	W-E STUNTS 420-418
2	W-F LEAD-UPS 508-517	W-A STUNTS 361-368-366	W-B MOVEMENT 48-65	W-C RHYTHMS 222-224	W-D LEAD-UPS Page 123
3	W-E FITNESS Pages 123, 124	W-F MOVEMENT 46-59	W-A GAMES 92	W-B LEAD-UPS Pages 123, 124	W-C RHYTHMS 249-261
4	W-D STUNTS 308-305-338	W-E LEAD-UPS 508-517	W-F FITNESS 25	W-A GAMES 152-512	W-B RHYTHMS 273
5	W-C MOVEMENT 48-60	W-D STUNTS 287-328-348	W-E RHYTHMS 253-224	W-F FITNESS 34	W-A LEAD-UPS Pages 123, 124
6	W-B LEAD-UPS Play Softball	W-C RHYTHMS 273	W-D STUNTS 368-374-287	W-E MOVEMENT 52-53	W-F LEAD-UPS Play Softball
7	W-A RHYTHMS 249-261	W-B STUNTS 414-432	W-C LEAD-UPS Play Softball	W-D MOVEMENT 62-57	W-E GAMES 159-150
8	W-F STUNTS 305-308-322-366	W-A LEAD-UPS Play Softball	W-B LEAD-UPS Play Softball	W-C RHYTHMS 237-267	W-D LEAD-UPS Play Softball
9	W-E RHYTHMS 212-225	W-F FITNESS 348-361-366-412	W-A LEAD-UPS Play Softball	W-B LEAD-UPS Play Softball	W-C LEAD-UPS Play Softball

GRADE 5 — QUARTER 1

Week	Session 1	Session 2	Session 3	Session 4	Session 5
1	* W-A GAMES 110	W-B ATHLETICS Pages 121, 122	W-C GAMES 117	W-D RHYTHMS 221	W-E MOVEMENT 15-16
2	W-F FITNESS 519-521	W-A FITNESS 518-519-520	W-B GAMES 144-162	W-C FITNESS 348-361 366-412	W-D ATHLETICS Page 121
3	W-E ATHLETICS Pages 118, 119	W-F GAMES 110-135	W-A ATHLETICS Pages 118, 119	W-B STUNTS Choice	W-C MOVEMENT 18-19
4	W-D STUNTS 287-302 373-383	W-E ATHLETICS Pages 118, 119	W-F RHYTHMS 221	W-A ATHLETICS 107 Pages 121, 122	W-B ATHLETICS 140-148-128
5	W-C MOVEMENT 21-22	W-D ATHLETICS Page 119	W-E GAMES 89-138	W-F ATHLETICS 509 Pages 118, 119	W-A STUNTS 302-317-318
6	W-B RHYTHMS 273	W-C GAMES 190-509	W-D STUNTS 280-358-300	W-E GAMES 119-155	W-F MOVEMENT 23-24
7	W-A ATHLETICS Pages 121, 122	W-B MOVEMENT 12	W-C STUNTS 278-298-410	W-D RHYTHMS 271	W-E FITNESS 412-348 361-366
8	W-F MOVEMENT 25	W-A RHYTHMS 252	W-B ATHLETICS Play Touch Football	W-C STUNTS 376-365-364	W-D ATHLETICS Page 119
9	W-E RHYTHMS 259	W-F ATHLETICS Pages 118, 119	W-A STUNTS 390-296-391	W-B MOVEMENT 28	W-C RHYTHMS 252-228

GRADE 5 — QUARTER 2

Week	Session 1	Session 2	Session 3	Session 4	Session 5
1	* W-A FITNESS 374-373-361	W-B RHYTHMS 258	W-C STUNTS 362-325-328	W-D MOVEMENT 29-50	W-E RHYTHMS 259
2	W-F GAMES 89-139	W-A STUNTS 316-324-302	W-B RHYTHMS 228-252	W-C MOVEMENT 30-53-63	W-D FITNESS 521
3	W-E MOVEMENT 31-32-52	W-F RHYTHMS 230-273	W-A STUNTS 351-318-357	W-B FITNESS 522-518	W-C RHYTHMS 252-235
4	W-D ATHLETICS 451 Pages 115, 116	W-E GAMES 81-127	W-F STUNTS 348-361-359	W-A RHYTHMS 197-211	W-B MOVEMENT 46-47-49
5	W-C STUNTS 285-303-351	W-D ATHLETICS Page 117	W-E ATHLETICS 98 Page 117	W-F FITNESS 348-361 366-412	W-A RHYTHMS 260-228
6	W-B ATHLETICS 173	W-C STUNTS 371-286-278	W-D RHYTHMS 263-236	W-E MOVEMENT 55-38-39	W-F ATHLETICS 513 Page 115
7	W-A ATHLETICS 73-98	W-B GAMES 173-123	W-C ATHLETICS 123	W-D RHYTHMS 260-211	W-E FITNESS 190-519
8	W-F STUNTS 298-313	W-A RHYTHMS 263-244	W-B ATHLETICS 157	W-C ATHLETICS 141	W-D FITNESS 521-137
9	W-E RHYTHMS 236-244	W-F MOVEMENT 45-57-58	W-A GAMES 96	W-B GAMES 515	W-C GAMES 96

GRADE 5 — QUARTER 3

Week	Session 1	Session 2	Session 3	Session 4	Session 5
1	* W-A GAMES 101-139	W-B GAMES 96	W-C MOVEMENT 29-68-30	W-D RHYTHMS 228	W-E FITNESS 348-361 366-412
2	W-F MOVEMENT 31-32-50	W-A STUNTS 317-325-357	W-B GAMES 516	W-C GAMES 516-515	W-D RHYTHMS 228-235
3	W-E STUNTS 354-300-299	W-F ATHLETICS Page 120	W-A RHYTHMS 197-230	W-B FITNESS 518-522	W-C RHYTHMS 235-211
4	W-D ATHLETICS Pages 115, 116	W-E RHYTHMS 211-260	W-F MOVEMENT 51-52-53	W-A STUNTS 294-348-361	W-B GAMES 98
5	W-C RHYTHMS 260-263	W-D GAMES 173	W-E FITNESS 37	W-F GAMES 89-87	W-A MOVEMENT 38-54-55
6	W-B ATHLETICS 513	W-C STUNTS 361-362-355	W-D RHYTHMS 263-236	W-E FITNESS 361-294-295	W-F GAMES 73-138
7	W-A ATHLETICS Play Basketball	W-B RHYTHMS 230-197	W-C MOVEMENT 39-40-41	W-D STUNTS 294-404-292	W-E RHYTHMS 236-244
8	W-F MOVEMENT 61-62-63	W-A GAMES Play Basketball	W-B STUNTS 300-325-359	W-C GAMES 513-73	W-D RHYTHMS 244-228
9	W-E RHYTHMS 235-211	W-F GAMES 81-138	W-A GAMES 110-190	W-B FITNESS 522-412	W-C MOVEMENT 45-46-47

GRADE 5 — QUARTER 4

Week	Session 1	Session 2	Session 3	Session 4	Session 5
1	* W-A MOVEMENT 48-49-56	W-B STUNTS 328-325-329	W-C RHYTHMS 260-263	W-D GAMES 510-512	W-E GAMES 139
2	W-F FITNESS 371-374-375	W-A RHYTHMS 236-244	W-B GAMES 89-190	W-C GAMES 509	W-D STUNTS 300-370-371
3	W-E GAMES 511	W-F MOVEMENT 29-50-31	W-A GAMES 508	W-B RHYTHMS 228-235	W-C STUNTS 370-352-351
4	W-D RHYTHMS 211-260	W-E GAMES 109-110	W-F MOVEMENT 38-54-52	W-A STUNTS 303-324-410	W-B GAMES 81
5	W-C STUNTS 370-357-353	W-D RHYTHMS 263-236	W-E MOVEMENT 40-61-63	W-F GAMES 191-511	W-A GAMES 509
6	W-B RHYTHMS 244	W-C GAMES 523	W-D GAMES 127-166	W-E GAMES 80	W-F STUNTS 302-303-409
7	W-A ATHLETICS Pages 123, 124	W-B MOVEMENT 28-46-48	W-C RHYTHMS Choice	W-D GAMES 183-191	W-E ATHLETICS Pages 123, 124
8	W-F GAMES 162-163	W-A FITNESS 521-522	W-B FITNESS 524-525	W-C MOVEMENT 30-32-68	W-D FITNESS 520-519
9	W-E STUNTS 322-285-325	W-F MOVEMENT 51-53-55	W-A GAMES 143	W-B GAMES 171-134	W-C GAMES 103-140

GRADE 6 — QUARTER 1

Week	Session 1	Session 2	Session 3	Session 4	Session 5
1	* W-A MOVEMENT 38	W-B GAMES Choice	W-C RELAY 414-416	W-D FITNESS 526	W-E RELAY 492-493
2	W-F RELAY 421-426	W-A RHYTHMS 197	W-B MOVEMENT 11	W-C RHYTHMS 221	W-D STUNTS 294-360-394
3	W-E MOVMENT 29	W-F FITNESS 518-522-524	W-A GAMES 126-127	W-B RELAY 508	W-C RELAY 497-491
4	W-D RELAY 517	W-E RHYTHMS 221	W-F MOVEMENT 38-39-40-41	W-A RHYTHMS 241	W-B STUNTS 307-400-334
5	W-C RELAY 415	W-D GAMES 91	W-E FITNESS 525-523	W-F MOVEMENT 57-58	W-A RELAY 448-454
6	W-B RHYTHMS 259	W-C MOVEMENT 53	W-D ATHLETICS 494-495-498	W-E STUNTS 395-374	W-F RELAY 455-456
7	W-A FITNESS 519-520	W-B ATHLETICS 495-493	W-C GAMES 74	W-D STUNTS 292-336-337	W-E RELAY 414-420
8	W-F STUNTS 395-373-279	W-A RHYTHMS 221	W-B RELAY 448	W-C MOVEMENT 50-54	W-D RHYTHMS 266
9	W-E GAMES 95-514	W-F RELAY 421-439	W-A STUNTS 398-302-400	W-B RHYTHMS 248	W-C RHYTHMS 231

*W = Warm-up

GRADE 6 — QUARTER 2

Week	Session 1	Session 2	Session 3	Session 4	Session 5
1	* W-A STUNTS 285-397-312	W-B LEAD-UPS 429	W-C RELAY 459-460	W-D RHYTHMS 234	W-E RELAY 453-452
2	W-F MOVEMENT 52	W-A RELAY 417-416	W-B RHYTHMS 222	W-C RELAY 419-418	W-D STUNTS 386-289-404
3	W-E FITNESS 366-521	W-F RHYTHMS 273	W-A MOVEMENT 27	W-B RELAY 421-422	W-C STUNTS 395-318
4	W-D LEAD-UPS 164	W-E FITNESS 348-361 366-412	W-F MOVEMENT 26	W-A RHYTHMS 252	W-B RELAY 455
5	W-C RHYTHMS 228	W-D LEAD-UPS 107	W-E FITNESS 361-521	W-F RELAY 416-414	W-A RELAY 437-436
6	W-B LEAD-UPS 508-517	W-C RELAY 453-456	W-D STUNTS 332-333-335	W-E RHYTHMS 228-252	W-F STUNTS 322-325-329
7	W-A STUNTS 337-341-396	W-B MOVEMENT 60	W-C RELAY 414-420	W-D RHYTHMS 215	W-E RELAY 429-430
8	W-F RHYTHMS 203	W-A FITNESS 522-518	W-B MOVEMENT 45	W-C RELAY 429	W-D STUNTS 332-336
9	W-E RELAY 429	W-F RHYTHMS 215	W-A FITNESS 524-294-292	W-B MOVEMENT 28	W-C MOVEMENT 28

*W = Warm-up

GRADE 6 — QUARTER 3

Week	Session 1	Session 2	Session 3	Session 4	Session 5
1	* W-A RELAY 458-457	W-B MOVEMENT 31-32	W-C RELAY Choice	W-D RHYTHMS 274	W-E STUNTS 285-300-362
2	W-F STUNTS 361-400-292	W-A RHYTHMS 272	W-B MOVEMENT 52	W-C RELAY 448-421	W-D FITNESS 523-522
3	W-E RHYTHMS 274	W-F RELAY 429	W-A MOVEMENT 55	W-B FITNESS 521-415	W-C STUNTS 316-319-380
4	W-D MOVEMENT 38-39	W-E STUNTS 321-320-314	W-F RHYTHMS 258	W-A ATHLETICS 486-487-488	W-B FITNESS 322-361-279
5	W-C ATHLETICS 489-490-488	W-D FITNESS 348-303-422	W-E STUNTS 413-369	W-F RHYTHMS 197	W-A RELAY 141-157
6	W-B MOVEMENT 41	W-C RHYTHMS 252	W-D RELAY 157	W-E STUNTS 388-389	W-F LEAD-UPS 508-143
7	W-A LEAD-UPS 171	W-B RELAY 414-515	W-C RELAY Page 120	W-D RHYTHMS 252-248	W-E LEAD-UPS 186-171
8	W-F ATHLETICS Page 115	W-A RHYTHMS 225	W-B FITNESS 513	W-C MOVEMENT 40-61	W-D STUNTS 354-363-402
9	W-E RHYTHMS 271	W-F ATHLETICS Page 115	W-A LEAD-UPS 180-191	W-B MOVEMENT 48	W-C ATHLETICS Page 115

*W = Warm-up

GRADE 6 — QUARTER 4

Week	Session 1	Session 2	Session 3	Session 4	Session 5
1	* W-A FITNESS 524-525	W-B LEAD-UPS 510	W-C RELAY 140	W-D RHYTHMS 215	W-E STUNTS 289-374-377
2	W-F STUNTS 384-395-397	W-A ATHLETICS 173	W-B MOVEMENT 32	W-C RELAY 513	W-D RHYTHMS 258
3	W-E LEAD-UPS 79	W-F RHYTHMS 197	W-A FITNESS 521-518	W-B RELAY 162	W-C STUNTS 360-359-312
4	W-D MOVEMENT 49	W-E RELAY 121	W-F RHYTHMS 266	W-A MOVEMENT 46	W-B RELAY 173
5	W-C LEAD-UPS Play Softball	W-D FITNESS 361-366-434	W-E RELAY Page 121	W-F RHYTHMS 273	W-A RELAY Page 115
6	W-B RHYTHMS 252	W-C STUNTS 312-397	W-D RELAY 429	W-E MOVEMENT 57	W-F STUNTS 316-331
7	W-A RELAY 516	W-B LEAD-UPS 143	W-C RHYTHMS 203-265	W-D MOVEMENT 59	W-E RELAY Page 116
8	W-F RHYTHMS 224-274	W-A RELAY 429	W-B LEAD-UPS 515-511	W-C RELAY 157	W-D MOVEMENT 60
9	W-E STUNTS Choice	W-F FITNESS 526	W-A RHYTHMS 215	W-B MOVEMENT Review	W-C RELAY Choice

*W = Warm-up

Warm-Ups and Movement Exploration

1. Open each class with listed warm-up for day's lesson—3-5 minutes duration.

2. Have students repeat suggested activities at different speeds and levels.

3. Music can accompany warm-ups.

4. Teacher can add warm-ups using creative aspects pertaining to daily units of classroom curriculum, for example, water in different forms—snow, ice, rain, etc.

Warm-Ups

A. Students run about the room using all the space. Stop on signal (whistle, voice, etc.)
   1. On signal, run, jump, and land on feet. Stop on signal.
   2. Run, jump, and land on two feet.
   3. Run, jump, and land on two feet and two hands.
   4. Hop on two feet and stop and go on signal.

B. Find a space on the floor and lie on your back.
   1. Curl into the shape of a ball; hands grasp legs to your chest.
   2. Stretch from this curled shape into shape with arms over head spread wide and legs spread apart very wide.
   3. Repeat from small to large to small.
      a. very fast
      b. very slowly
      c. repeat

C. Students run and jump about the room.
   1. Twist body one-half turn to the right, run and twist one-half turn to left; continue running.
   2. Twist body a full turn and face original direction.
   3. Run and do one-half twists and full body twists thrusting arms over head and spreading legs wide.

D. Students stand on floor.
   1. With legs together and feet firmly planted, walk hands around to either side on floor until they can go no further and walk them back.
   2. Spread your feet very wide; don't move feet. Reach through your legs as far to the rear as possible and touch the floor.
   3. Reach as far as possible in front of you and touch the floor.
   4. With your hands and feet on the floor, kick your legs backward and up into the air. Repeat 5-10 times.

E. Students lie on the floor face up to sky.
   1. Roll to the right side with hands over the head and roll back to first position.
   2. Do the same to the left side.
   3. Roll all the way over and back to first position.
   4. Stand up fast.
   5. Lie down fast on your stomach.

F. Students lie on the floor face down.
   1. Place your hands and feet on the floor with wide spread legs and hands. Raise body off floor with feet and hands only touching floor. Walk in this position in your space.
   2. Roll over on your back and raise body off the floor with only the hands and feet touching the floor. Walk in this position in your space.
   3. Alternate these two stunts.

Movement Exploration

1—Who can show me
1. how far he can stretch out?
2. what his hands do?
3. how tall he can be?
4. how his hands can lead him to the wall and back?
5. how one hand can lead, now the other one?
6. how his right hand can take him in a small circle, then the left hand?
7. how each hand can take him in a larger circle?

2—Who can
1. make his hands move quickly?
2. make his hands move slowly?
3. show me how strong he is?
4. make his hands strong and quick?
5. make his whole body strong and quick?
6. make his hands light and quick?
7. make his whole body light and quick?

3—Can you
1. show me the shape of the space in which you live?
2. try painting it all different colors, behind you, in front of you, all around you?

4—Can you
1. make a new space and show me how small it is?
2. make it get larger . . . higher . . . wider?
3. paint in lots of colors and make the biggest space you ever saw?

5—Show me
1. how a top spins.
2. how to wind up all the tops and pull the strings.
3. who can wind us up and make us go the other way around.
4. how you can make your elbow twist you down to the floor with a strong twist.
5. how your other elbow can unscrew you again.

6—Who can
1. do a quick, light movement very high?
2. do a quick, strong movement that goes from middle to low?
3. try both movements, one after the other (high to low)?
4. try this with a partner (one does the movement for the other)?

7—How do

1. people look and walk when they are going out of the field house after a basketball game?
2. they look and walk if they have lost the game? won the game?
3. you show people if you have won or lost the game?

8—Who can

1. go and touch the nearest wall and come back to his space without touching anything else?
2. touch the top of his space?
3. touch the front of his space?
4. touch the back of his space without moving his feet?
5. show how far his space stretches from his feet? from his waist? above his head?

9—Can you

1. point to a spot a long way from your own space, run to it as fast as you can, and stop on it?
2. come back to your own space as fast as you can?
3. make your feet move fast right in your own space?
4. move even faster in your own space but not standing on your feet?
5. make your arms move fast?
6. make your arms and feet move fast?
7. go to the same spot as you did before, and come back again, moving both arms and feet very fast?

10—Let us try

1. to stretch both arms.
2. to stretch both feet.
3. to squeeze ourselves until we are very small.
4. to stretch out until we are very wide.
5. to be very tall and thin.

11—Let's see

1. if your feet can take you in a small circle right in your own space.
2. what else they can do besides walk and run. (jump, skip, gallop, hop)
3. how many things they can do while they take you to the wall and back.
4. if they can go higher than your head.
5. if they can go right in front of your head. behind your head.

2

12—Can you

1. grip hard with your feet and legs while you go to each corner of the room and back again to your own space without touching any other child?
2. keep gripping and try to make your feet and legs slow and strong?
3. make your hands strong and slow?
4. show me how you feel when your hands and feet are strong and slow.
5. do strong, slow movements and show me by your faces how you feel?
6. do light, slow movements?
7. do light, slow movements with your hands and feet?
8. show how you feel when you do this?
9. let your hands move lightly and quickly?
10. make your hands go right down to the floor?
11. pat the floor lightly and quickly?
12. make your hands go high with quick, light movements?
13. go up in the air higher still?
14. make quick little jumps with both hands and feet?
15. bring your hands down to middle height but still make light and quick movements?
16. jump with your hands on your hips?
17. jump high and light?
18. children who are wearing something red sit down and watch the others jump high and light?
19. tell me what you liked?
20. children wearing red jump now and the others sit down and watch?
21. tell me what you noticed?

13—Will you

1. lean forward as far as you can without falling?
2. tell me what your feet do?
3. try the same thing sideways?
4. tell us what rule of balance you discovered? (Keep your feet directly under your weight.)
5. show us another rule?
   a. Take a partner, grasp his right hand, brace your right feet against each other.
   b. Try to keep your own feet while you push and pull your partner so he has to move his feet.
6. try different positions of your feet, always keeping your right foot braced against your partner's right foot?
7. make another rule? (The lower your weight, the better your balance.)
8. try balancing on one part of your body? now on two parts? Which is easier?

14—Can you

practice tiptoeing?
   a. fast?
   b. slowly?
   c. strong?
   d. high?
   e. very lightly?

15—Would you in your group

1. pick a goal?
2. try walking around in a circle and moving forward at the same time?
3. try the same thing running?

16—Can you

1. have one team be "it"?
2. get a ball and take it to your common space?
3. play the ball only with your feet?
4. try to keep the ball while the "it" team tries to get it away?
   a. If they get the ball —you become "it."
   b. If you touch someone else, you are "dead" and have to come over to the side and practice noninterference.

17—Let's try

1. doing this with partners.
2. throwing hard.
3. catching the ball on the first bounce.
4. not getting too excited.

18—Can you

1. write a number in the air with your arm?
2. put the same number on the floor while running?
3. take a partner, run your number on the floor, and let your partner guess what it is. Take turns.

19—Try

1. having your elbow lead you to the wall and back.
2. having your chest lead you to the wall.
3. having your back lead you back to your space.
4. it again, chest leading to the wall, back leading back.
5. standing on your hands and knees, and seeing how high your back can go and how low it can go.
6. to hump it up . . . make it hollow.
7. to sit back on your heels, and see whether you can hump your back and then hollow it. (Note what happens to the chest each time.)
8. to take out the hollow, straighten your back, and still keep your chest high.
9. standing, and take out the hollow, straighten your back, and keep your chest high. Walk lightly around, keeping tall.

20—Can you

1. do a strong, quick movement using arms and legs in straight lines out and in?
2. have your legs do what they did before while you make your arms go straight up and down?
3. make your legs go straight up and down?
4. do any kind of **slow** movement in your own space while making curved lines first with arms, then with legs, then with body?

21—How would you

1. make yourself very small?
2. roll like a ball?
3. roll around in your space?
4. stand up and show me with your arms where you went when you rolled like a ball?
5. stand in your space and make a circle?

22—Can you

1. make your feet take you around the floor in a big circle?
2. see whether some of you can go in the same circle?
3. make another circle?
4. go around in the circle and try to see what different things your feet will do?
5. go the other way in your circle and try to do different things?

4

23—Can you

1. move your feet very fast, right where you are?
2. sit down and see how many ways your feet can move (bend and stretch and roll around the ankle)?
3. do little jumps in your own space and think what your feet do?
4. try it again and see what else bends and stretches?
5. see if your feet can take you in a circle, and do all the things you did last time.
   (Use same approach to explain use of hands.)

24—Let's try

1. to see how thin we can make ourselves.
2. to make ourselves look like sticks, boards, arrows.
3. to show how an arrow goes through the air.
4. to make our arrows go again but all in the same way.
5. to make our arrows go the other way.
6. to show what an arrow would look like when it stops.

25—Who can

1. move fast and stop suddenly like a bicycle? a pony? a fish? an animal? a car? a football player?
2. run very fast and stop suddenly when he hears the whistle?
3. run fast in one direction, stop suddenly and then run in another direction?
4. run and stop suddenly without any signal?

26—Would you

1. try drawing some movements on the board that we could demonstrate by moving around the gym?
2. show how your group is working out the design? (Evaluate with group.)

27—During the summer, I am sure all of you went on a picnic with your family.

Who can

show by his movements what he did at the picnic (circus, zoo, airport, railroad station, baseball games)?

28—Who can

1. sit in his space and count the number of joints in his body that he can touch?
2. bend all the joints in his hips, legs and feet, both legs working together?
3. see how far he can stretch his hips, legs, feet, both legs stretching together?
4. stretch his shoulders, arms, hands, fingers?
5. bend and stretch his spine?
6. see all the things his spine can do?
7. run lightly and not too fast anywhere in the gym, and notice if his arms and legs are bending or stretching?
8. skip . . . gallop . . . run to his own space?
9. run to see what his spine does?
10. touch the floor without bending his knees?
11. keep his spine straight and bend just at the hips?

29—Can you

1. make straight lines while running quickly and lightly?
2. change your direction but still keep running in a straight line?
3. take a partner and run making the letter Z?
4. do a light, quick walk?
   (Remember that **direct** means straight movement; **indirect** is curved.)
5. give me a direct movement with your arms? elbows?
6. give me an indirect movement with your arms? body?
7. twist and turn your body?

30—Will you

1. walk to the black line, run to the white line, and stop?
2. turn and run to the black line?
3. remember to stop with your feet apart?
4. remember to begin running with short, quick, strong steps?
5. run very fast in a zigzag pattern?

31—Try to

1. take a partner and work out some movement patterns.
2. do a quick, light, direct movement.
3. do a quick, strong, direct movement.
4. do your movement patterns alternately.

32—Show me

1. slow, indirect, light movements.
2. slow, indirect, strong movements.
3. changing levels in the two patterns.
4. different speeds in the two patterns.

33—Show me

1. your knees.
2. how high they can go . . . how low . . . how far apart . . . how close together.
3. if they can go higher then your hips (jumping).
4. whether you can run very fast and then let both knees go very high at once.
5. how you can move very slowly, letting first one knee, then the other, go high (gallop, skip).
6. what your knees do when you try to see how tall and thin you can be.
7. what your knees do when you move at a very low level . . . when you are in between.

34—Let's try

1. a slow, strong movement using your whole body: hands, elbows, knees, feet.
2. a slow, light movement.
3. a slow, strong movement first, then a slow light movement.
4. doing a slow, strong movement with a partner.
5. doing a slow, light movement with a partner.
6. changing from one to the other, without stopping.

35—Who can

1. do a strong, quick movement while his partner watches? (Reverse the procedure.)
2. try a quick, light movement, first one partner, then the other?

36—Can you

1. squat down in your space and show me what your elbow can do?
2. move your elbow up? down? forward? backward? around in a circle?
3. make your body move with your elbow?
4. show how far around to the back your left elbow will move? your right elbow?
5. move your elbow up? How high can it go?
6. let your elbow pull you to the nearest wall?
7. see if your elbow will turn you around and lead you back?
8. make your elbow pull you to the wall, turn you around and bring you back?

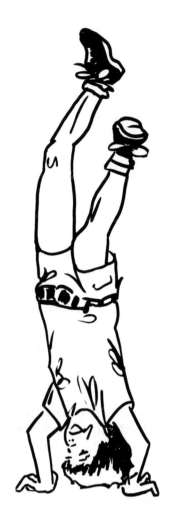

37—Try to

1. crawl as close to the ground as you can.
2. crawl like a snake, a spider, a worm.
3. show how tall you can be.
4. walk like a boy on stilts, a giant, a long-legged clown.
5. go way up when you run, skip, walk.
6. walk and change levels when I give the signal—high, low, middle, high, low, high.
7. face a partner, join both hands, stay in the same place and change levels; however, when one goes up the other must go down.

39—Let us try

1. to press hard on the wall using direct, slow, and strong movements.
2. to dance lightly on the floor using direct, quick, and light movements.
3. to be a bulldozer (push hard).
4. to lightly bounce a ball.

40—Can you

1. dance and swing your arms at the same time?
2. push on the wall with one hand and bounce a ball with the other?
3. jump lightly and clap your hands at the same time?
4. swing your arm in a circle?

38—Let us try

1. to punch at the air using direct, quick, and strong movements.
2. to hit a fly using indirect, quick, and strong movements.
3. to jump very far.
4. to jump very high.

41—Who can
1. float in the air like a feather?
2. act like an airplane in the wind?
3. act like mother sweeping the floor?
4. squeeze his hands really tight?

42—Can you
1. crouch down close to the ground, keeping on your feet?
2. shoot your arms out fast, wide apart . . . do it again?
3. shoot both arms and legs out, quickly as you can and far apart?
4. do something else that is a quick, strong movement?
5. do something that is a quick, light movement?
6. do your quick, strong movement, stop still, and then do your quick, light movement several times?
7. do a quick, light movement, then a quick, strong movement several times?

43—Show me
1. on the chalkboard just where the jet plane went.
2. with your arms in the air where the jet plane went.
3. this same path of the jet across the gym.
4. on the floor, ways other planes go in the sky; in a little space with your finger; now so big you go all over the gym.

44—Can you
1. take a trip across the gym and back, using both plane and car (auto, plane, ocean liner, speedboat, submarine)?
2. take a trip all around the gym and change from one thing to another?
3. take another trip and let us guess what you are traveling in?

45—Let's try
1. moving our bodies in our own spaces.
2. combining three movements and making a nice pattern.
3. balancing on four, three, two, then one part of our bodies.
4. three nonlocomotor movements and finish with a balance on three points.

46—Let's see
1. one of you do strong movements.
2. someone else reply with light movements.
3. two of you do the same movement, only differ in strength.

47—Can you
1. think and move like characters in a crowd?
2. move your shoulders like a performer on the high wire?
3. act like a lion tamer?

48—Show me
1. at least two different patterns you have learned.
2. one pattern in two ways.
3. your partner's pattern.
4. one other pattern twice.

49—Would you
show us how these people act?
    a. tired travelers
    b. the team that won
    c. the team that lost
    d. strangers in the city
    e. nervous parents

50—Let's try

1. acting like a batter.
2. acting like a coach.
3. looking at a ball in the air.
4. running to a base.
5. to watch both the runner and the base.

51—Can you

1. join hands with a leader at one end?
2. move along together at a light walk?
3. watch to see what the leader is looking at?
4. move toward what he is looking at?
5. remember the story "_____" you read last?
6. act out a scene?

52—Will you

1. make a pattern of quick, indirect, light movements?
2. make a pattern of quick, direct, light movements?
3. try to use different floor patterns?
4. use many parts of your body in a pattern?
5. try changing the focus from one pattern to another?

53—Who can

1. put his feet together, straighten his knees, bend forward, and touch the floor?
2. bob up and down?
3. put his arms horizontal, feet apart, bend and twist to touch his left foot with his right hand?
4. put his arms horizontal, feet apart, bend and twist to touch his right foot with his left hand? sit with his feet apart, bend forward to touch his left foot with the right hand?
5. sit with his feet apart, bend forward to touch his right foot with the left hand?
6. sit with his feet apart, bend forward to touch his right foot with the left hand?
7. come toward me with long, light, leaping steps?
8. back away with small steps?

54—Can you

1. make quick, indirect, light movements followed by quick, direct, light movements?
2. make different floor patterns?
3. make some large movements?
4. make some small movements?
5. make some wide movements?
6. make some narrow movements?

55—Let's see

1. a direct, quick, strong movement.
2. an indirect, quick, strong movement.
3. a direct, quick, strong movement.
4. a direct, slow, strong movement.
5. a direct, quick, strong movement.
6. a direct, quick, light movement.
7. whether you can move through the six parts without stopping.

56—Can you take a partner and

1. do a pattern with him replying?
2. change as many qualities as you wish?
3. do the same pattern your partner does?
4. do a floating pattern?
5. do a snap pattern?

57—How would you take a partner and

1. try many different kinds of steps?
   a. running
   b. skipping
   c. leaping
   d. hopping
   e. galloping
   f. sliding
2. join with two others and do all the above steps together?
3. skip and skip and run, run, run?
4. play an instrument while keeping in step?

58—Can you in your group

1. get a musical instrument?
2. skip and beat out the accompaniment?
3. try
   a. gallop?
   b. slide and slide?
   c. three runs and a hop?
   d. three skips and a jump?
   e. making up some of your own patterns?
4. change the range of your movements as you do the pattern?
5. change the focus as you do the pattern?
6. try a nonlocomotor movement
   a. push
   b. pull
   c. swing

59—Would you

1. do a strong, quick, indirect movement?
2. do a strong, slow, direct movement?
3. repeat your patterns several times so we can all beat rhythm to it?
4. beat time on an instrument to accompany your pattern?

60—Will you and your group

1. choose a phrase to work on?
   a. Will you help me?
   b. I'm stronger than you are.
   c. Let's be friends.
   d. Catch the thieves!
   e. Don't be afraid!
   f. Let's find out.
2. express this phrase to each other?
3. use all the things you know?
   a. feelings   d. floor patterns
   b. levels   e. range
   c. focus   f. variety of movement

61—Let's see

1. if you can run and jump at the same time.
2. if you can run and jump and clap your hands at the same time.
3. if you can jump, then run, then clap your hands.
4. if you can clap your hands, then jump, then run.

62—Try to

1. feel relaxed . . . float.
2. feel mysterious . . . glide around.
3. feel uneasy . . . toss about.
4. feel itchy about something . . . wiggle around.

10

63—Who can

1. take four walks, two hops, and a jump?
2. take four gallops, two leaps, and a jump?
3. lean forward a little on gallops and jumps?
4. run to the black line and then back to the white line?
5. run straight forward, touch the black line with one foot, then run to your right without losing balance?

64—Shall we

1. see how light our landing can be?
2. do small jumps in our own space?
3. do them so lightly we can't hear them?
4. do three small jumps and one high jump?
5. discuss how we made the high jump?
6. try it all over again?

65—Let's try

1. to curl up, bending in all our joints.
2. to stretch out, slowly.
3. it from a different position, keeping both bending and stretching slow.
4. to curl up slowly, then stretch out as fast as we can.
5. this in three parts:
   a. curl up slowly.
   b. shoot out as wide and fast as we can.
   c. relax easily and quickly, right down to the floor.
6. to repeat the three parts slowly and lightly, quickly and strongly, quickly and lightly.

66—Can you

1. look in as many directions as you can without moving your feet?
2. let your feet move, turning you around in your space until you are back where you started?
3. try it a little faster?
4. go around the other way?
5. do a hard pattern?

67—Let's see

1. if your spine bends as you walk.
2. you stop in your space and relax slowly until you are on the floor; then lie in relaxed position.
3. what has to work when you get up and stand tall. (Muscles. Why do your muscles have to work against your weight? gravity. Good posture is a sign of strength, balance, and flexibility.)
4. you try walking in good posture.

68—Who can

1. move like a fish or snake?
2. move like a cat or dog?
3. move like an ape?
4. move like a human being, both fast and slow?
5. see how many kinds of steps he can use with a partner?
6. watch his partner going through each stage, beginning without any arms or legs?
7. tell which boys and girls looked most like humans? (They are tall, hold heads high, stand easy, but erect.)
8. sit down like apes?
9. sit down like humans?

69—In your own space, can you

1. let your left elbow take you in a very small circle?
2. make your right elbow do the same?
3. show how your nose leads you to a corner of the gym and back?
4. let your nose take you all around this room?
5. have your hips lead you backward and then forward?
6. move your hips to the left without moving your feet? to the right?
7. make a circle with your hips while your feet stand still and your head stays in the same place?
8. try the same thing but go the other way around?
9. get your hips higher than your head?

70—Can you

1. sit down in your own space and put your feet straight out in front of you?
2. stretch your toes very far?
3. see how far back you can bend?
4. bend your feet so far back that your toes are farther back than your heels?
5. move your toes forward and backward?
6. lie on your back and put your feet in the air?
7. show how high your toes will reach? your heels?
8. get your heels higher than your toes?
9. lie on your back and move your feet quickly and lightly?
10. make a tiny circle in the air with your left toes?
11. make a larger circle?
12. do the same with your right toes? both sets of toes? both heels?
13. walk to the wall and back on your heels?
14. do the same on your toes?
15. run, skip, gallop, hop, leap?
16. go sideways with one foot following the other and do just what the first foot does?
17. go the other way with the other foot going first?
18. do five slides right and then five slides left?
19. hop, slide and slide, hop, slide and slide?

Teacher Notes

12

Games

71—Animal Chase

Playing Area: Playground. Two parallel lines are drawn 50 feet apart. Halfway between the lines and off to one side, a rectangle represents the zoo.

Players: Entire class

Equipment: None

1. The hunter stands in the center of the playing area. The other children stand behind one of two goal lines. Each secretly chooses an animal (several children with the same name will make the game more exciting).
2. When the hunter calls out the name of an animal, the child with that name must run to the opposite goal line and return before being tagged by the hunter.
3. The hunter, after calling, must run to the zoo, get his gun, return to his center position, and try to tag the runner.
4. If an animal is tagged, he is taken to the zoo where he remains until all have run or been tagged.

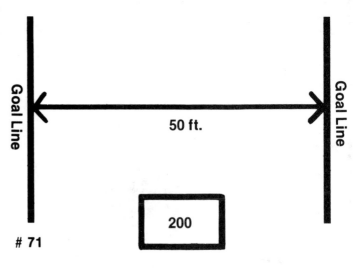

71

73—Around the Key

Playing Area: One end of a basketball court. Spots are indicated in the diagram.

Players: 3 to 8 players

Equipment: Basketball

1. A player begins in the first position and continues to shoot as long as he makes the shot.
2. If he fails to make the shot, he has one of two choices:
   a. wait for his next turn at the position from which he missed and then continue.
   b. take one more shot from where he missed. If he makes the shot, he may continue. If he misses he starts over from the beginning on his next turn.
3. The winner is the one who progresses the farthest or completes the key.

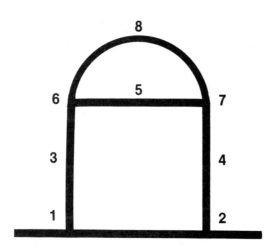

#73

72—Animal Tag

Playing Area: Playground or gym. Two parallel lines are drawn 40 feet apart.

Players: Entire class, divided into 2 groups

Equipment: None

1. Each group takes a position behind one of the lines.
2. Group 1 selects an animal to imitate. Once the selection is made, this group moves to within five feet of Group 2 which attempts to identify the animal by taking turns guessing.
3. If a correct guess is made, Group 2 chases Group 1 back to its line. Those tagged from Group 1 join Group 2.
4. Group 2 now selects an animal and goes through the same procedure.
5. If no one guesses correctly, the performing team receives another try.

74—Around the Row

Playing Area: Row in a classroom

Players: Number in a row

Equipment: None

1. Played somewhat like musical chairs, this game involves the children from one row of a classroom and one extra player. All quietly walk around their row when the teacher gives the appropriate indication: "March."
2. When the signal to stop is given, the children attempt to gain possession of one of the vacant seats.
3. One player will be without a seat; he then joins the next row of players as the game proceeds across the room.

75—Back to Back

Playing Area: Gym or playground
Players: Any number arranged in pairs
Equipment: None

1. Each child stands back to back with another child.
2. One player does not have a partner.
3. At the teacher's signal (whistle, hand clap, "Change!"), all players change partners while the extra player attempts to get a partner.
4. One player will be left without a partner each time. The game is repeated with this player giving the signal for the next change.

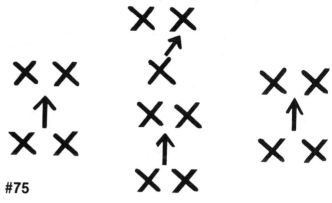

#75

76—Ball Carrying

Playing Area: Gym or playground. A field 30 by 60 yards is marked off in 20-yard intervals.
Players: 4 for each run
Equipment: Football, 2 flags for each player

1. Placed at 20-yard intervals and facing the goal line are three defensive players, each of whom is assigned to the zone he faces.
2. The defensive players must down the ball carrier, who stands ready to run at the goal line, by pulling a flag from the carrier while he is within a particular zone. If flags are not available, tag with two hands.
3. The ball carrier attempts to dodge each defender without having any of his flags pulled.
4. Should one of the flags be pulled from the carrier, he continues to run. If, however, the two flags are pulled, the last defender then uses a two-hand touch in downing the ball carrier.
5. After having completed his run, the runner proceeds to rotate into a defending position.

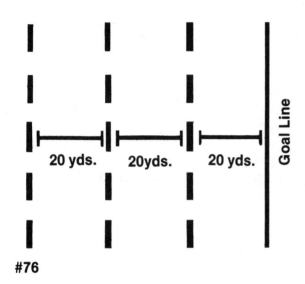

#76

77—Ball Exchange

Playing Area: Gym or playground
Players: 10 to 20
Equipment: Football

1. Arranged in a shuttle formation, the two halves of the shuttle face each other across a 15-yard distance. The head of one of the files carries the ball to the head of the other file and then joins the end of that file.
2. The ball is carried back and forth between the two files of the shuttle.
3. The receiving player should not start out until the carrier is almost to him.

78—Ball Passing

Playing Area: Playground or gym
Players: Entire class, divided into two or more teams
Equipment: 5 to 6 different kinds of balls for each circle

1. The teacher starts a ball around the circle; the ball is passed from player to player.
2. Eventually five or six balls are moving around the circle at one time.
3. Should any ball be dropped in its travels around the circle, the child who drops it immediately retrieves it and a point is scored against the team of which he is a member.
4. The lowest score wins the game.

#77

15

79—Ball Toss
Playing Area: Gym or playground
Players: Groups of 6 to 8
Equipment: Ball or beanbag for each group

1. The children form a circle with one child in the center of it.
2. The center player practices passing and catching with each player in the circle.
3. Each child should have a turn in the center. The teacher should stress form and the completion of as many throws and catches with as few errors as possible.

82—Beanbag Pitch
Playing Area: Classroom or gym
Players: 2 to 6 for each target
Equipment: Beanbags and a small box for each team

1. Approximately two to six players line up behind a line which is drawn ten to fifteen feet from a target box.
2. Each player is allowed to take a specified number of pitches to hit the box.
3. The score for each player is tallied and the team with the highest score wins.

80—Bat Ball
Playing Area: Gym or playground. A serving line is drawn across one end of a 70' by 70' field. A 3' x 3' base is drawn 50' from the serving line.
Players: Two teams, 8 to 15 on each
Equipment: Volley or similar ball

1. One captain arranges his players in the field while the other arranges his behind the serving line.
2. A player bats by throwing the ball in the air and hitting it with his hand.
3. If the ball does not go over the serving line or goes outside the playing area, it is a strike. Three strikes per player and three outs per team are allowed.
4. If the ball is fair, the batter must run to the base and back to the serving line before being hit below the shoulders by a player.
5. The ball must be thrown from fielder to fielder until thrown at the batter.
6. If the batter reaches the serving line without being hit, he scores a point. If hit by the ball, if the ball is caught on a fly, or if two consecutive fouls are made, the batter is out.
7. The team with the most points wins.

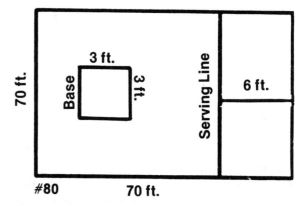

#80

81—Battle Dodgeball
Playing Area: Gym or playground
Players: Two teams
Equipment: 2 volleyballs or rubber balls

1. A circle is formed by two teams, each of which occupies one-half of the circle.
2. Players on each team are numbered.
3. A ball is placed, on each side of the center line, about five feet apart.
4. When a number is called, the two players with that number rush to their respective team's ball, throw and try to hit the other; each player must stay in his half of the circle.
5. Other players may retrieve balls and throw them back to their teammates in the center.
6. A point is scored when a player is hit; then another number is called.

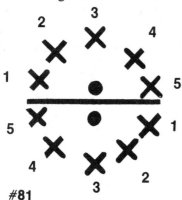

#81

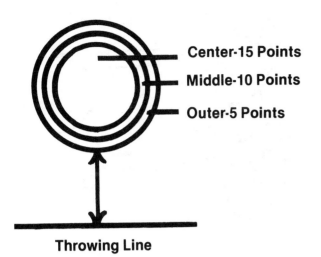

Center-15 Points

Middle-10 Points

Outer-5 Points

Throwing Line

#83

83—Beanbag Target Toss
Playing Area: Gym. Three concentric circles are drawn on the floor with radii of 10'', 20'', and 30''.
Players: 2 to 6 for each target
Equipment: 5 beanbags

1. Positioned ten to fifteen feet from the target, each player tosses five beanbags at the target.
2. Scoring is indicated in the diagram to the left.
3. To receive an area's score, the bag must be completely within the area. Any bag touching a line receives 3 points.
4. The score is determined by the position of the bags in the target area.

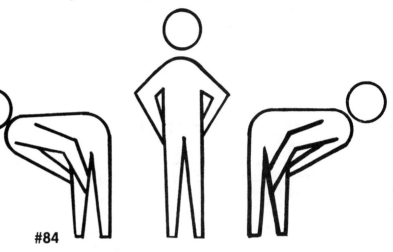

#84

84—The Bear Hug
Starting Position: Standing, feet comfortably spread, hands on hips

1. Pupil takes a long step diagonally right, keeping his left foot in place. He bends, tackles the right thigh with both arms, stretches and squeezes.
2. Returns to position.
3. Tackles the left leg.
4. Returns to position.

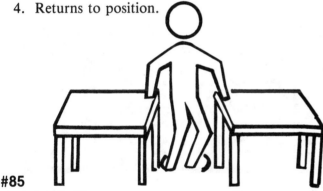

#85

85—Bicycle Race
Playing Area: Classroom
Players: One-half the class
Equipment: Desks

1. One-half of the class is used, allowing alternate rows to perform at one time.
2. Each child stands in the aisle between two desks, one hand on his own desk and his other hand on the neighboring desk.
3. On a signal from the teacher, the child supports himself on his hands while bicycling with his legs.
4. The child who is able to bicycle the longest, without allowing his feet to touch the floor, is the winner.

86—Birds Fly
Playing Area: Classroom
Players: Entire class
Equipment: None

1. A child stands in front of the other children as leader.
2. He proceeds to call out the names of things that can fly ("birds fly") and things that cannot fly ("lions fly"), always raising his arms in imitation of flying.
3. The other children raise their arms only when the leader names something that can fly. If any child raises his arms when something is named that cannot fly, that child must sit down.
4. The winner is that child who remains standing the longest.

 Leader

Children

#86

87—Black Bird

Playing Area: Gym
Players: Entire class
Equipment: None

1. The players are divided into two groups. Each group is behind one of two goal lines marked across opposite ends of the play area.
2. The player chosen as "it" stands in the middle of the playing area and calls "Black Bird!" (the signal for the players to change goals).
3. "It" attempts to tag a player before he is able to reach the opposite goal; if tagged, that player becomes "it" and the game is repeated.
4. Because the signal is "Black Bird!" any player who runs at a trick signal is immediately "it."

88—Boiler Burst

Playing Area: Gym or classroom
Players: Entire class
Equipment: None

1. The children are grouped around a player who begins a story.
2. When he calls, "Boiler Burst!" this is the signal that he is going to chase the other players, who run for the safety zone.
3. The first player caught starts the game again, with the players around him. The same story may be continued or a new one begun.

89—Bombardment

Playing Area: Gym
Players: Two teams, 10 to 15 on each team
Equipment: 12 Indian clubs for each team, 4 volley or soccer balls

1. Each team attempts to knock over the other team's clubs and at the same time protect their own clubs.
2. The captain and the one other player from each team, positioned near the center line, must bowl the balls at the other team's clubs; other players may catch the balls and throw them to those players nearer the front.
3. Players score fouls in these ways:
   a. going over the center line into the other team's space.
   b. running with the ball or dribbling it (it must be passed).
   c. throwing at a club from outside the side lines.
   d. holding the ball instead of throwing it.
   e. touching one of their clubs that has been knocked down.
4. The first team to successfully knock down all clubs on the opponent's side is declared winner.
5. Players who knock down clubs on their own team score a point for the opposing team.

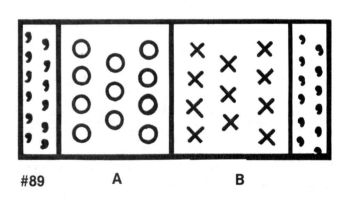

#89   A   B

90—Bounce Ball

Playing Area: 40' x 60' with center line
Players: Two teams, 8 to 15 players on each
Equipment: 2 volleyballs or rubber balls

1. Each team occupies one half of the court and is given a rubber ball.
2. Players attempt to bounce or roll their ball across the opponent's end line.
3. Players are allowed to move anywhere within their court half but may not cross the center line.
4. Each team should assign one or two ball retrievers and one scorer who are positioned at their respective end lines.

91—Bowling

Playing Area: Classroom (file by rows)

Players: 2 to 6

Equipment: Bowling pins and ball(s)

1. Using an aisle of the classroom as an alley, the pin (or pins) is placed at one end of the row.
2. A ball of adequate size is used to roll down the "alley" to hit the target.
3. Competition can be between rows or individuals within a row.

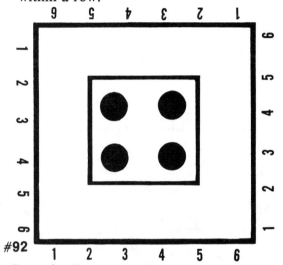

#92

93—Broncho Tag

Playing Area: Gym

Players: 15 to 30

Equipment: None

1. One child is the chaser and another the runner.
2. The remainder of the children, are divided into groups of three, forming a broncho by standing one behind the other and grasping the waist of the person in front.
3. The chaser pursures the runner who tries to hook on to the tail of any broncho.
4. The head of the broncho now becomes the runner.
5. The chaser pursues the new runner, who does the same as the original runner.
6. If the runner is tagged, he becomes the chaser and the chaser becomes the runner.

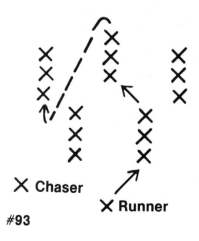

X Chaser

X Runner

#93

92—Box Ball

Playing Area: Gym

Players: Four teams, 6 to 10 on each

Equipment: Sturdy box. One ball for each team

1. Each team occupies one side of a square court at an equal distance from the center. Each team is facing inward and is numbered consecutively from left to right.
2. A box containing four balls is put in the center of the square.
3. The teacher calls a number and the players who have that number run to the center, take a ball from the box, and run to the head of their respective teams.
4. The other players move to the right just enough to fill the vacancy left by the runner.
5. The runner, once at the head of the team, passes the ball to the next player and so on down the line until it is caught by the last player on that team.
6. The end player then takes the ball and deposits it in the box.
7. The first team to return the ball to the box scores a point.

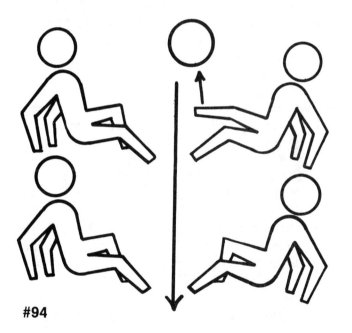

#94

94—Cage Ball Kickover

Playing Area: Gym

Players: Two teams, 7 to 10 on each

Equipment: A cageball (18, 24, or 30 inch)

1. Two teams sit facing each other with their legs outstretched. Each player supports his weight on his hands, which are placed slightly back of him.
2. The teacher rolls the cageball between the two teams. The object is to kick the ball over the heads of the opposing team.
3. No point is scored if the ball is kicked out either of the two ends.

19

95—Caged Lion

Playing Area: Classroom or gym. A ten-foot square
Players: 10 to 20
Equipment: None

1. One player is selected to be the "lion," and takes his position on hands and knees inside the square.
2. The other players run up to the "lion" and through his cage tempting him.
3. The "lion" tries to reach out and tag any one of the players tempting him.
4. Should a player be tagged by the "lion," that player takes the place of the "lion" in the cage.

96—Cage Volleyball

Playing Area: Gym
Players: Two teams, 6 to 9 each
Equipment: Net and cageball, 18 or 24-inch diameter

1. A variation of regular volleyball, the game is begun with a serve. The ball is tossed in the air and batted with both hands.
2. If necessary, assistance may be given in getting the ball over the net with any number of hits and by any player.
3. The server, the right back player, continues the serve and scores points until his team errs, at which time the ball goes to the opposing team.

97—Call Ball

Playing Area: Gym
Players: 6 to 8 in each circle
Equipment: Large ball or volleyball

1. One child in the center tosses the ball above his head while calling clearly the name of a child in the circle.
2. That child attempts to catch the ball before it bounces or before it bounces more than one time.
3. If he catches the ball, he takes the place of the child in the center of the circle and tosses the ball; however, if he fails to catch the ball, the child in the center remains until there has been a successful catch.

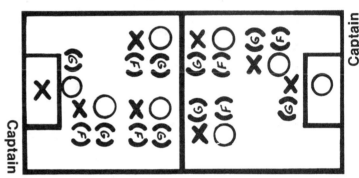

#98

98—Captain Basketball

Playing Area: Basketball court
Players: 6 or 8 on each team
Equipment: Basketball

1. The game is played much the same as basketball. A team consists of three forwards, four guards, and one captain.
2. The game begins with a jump ball, after which the ball is advanced. However, since no player may cross the center line, guards must maneuver the ball to the center line and pass it to one of their forwards. The forwards attempt to successfully complete a pass to their team's captain, who must remain stationed with one foot under the area of the basket.
3. Should a player step over the center line or a guard into the captain's area, the opposing team wins a free throw.
4. When a team wins a free throw, a forward stands at the free throw line and has five seconds to pass to his captain who is guarded by one player. If the pass is successful, the ball is in play again.
5. Points: a throw by a forward into the captain is 2 points; a free throw is 1 point.

99—Cat and Mice
Playing Area: Classroom
Players: 10 to 20
Equipment: None

1. One child, who is selected to be the cat, sits with his back to the other players, who sit in their seats.
2. The teacher chooses four or five mice and signals for them to quietly sneak up to the cat's hiding place and scratch on the desk or stool; this is a signal for the cat to chase the mice back to the safety of their holes (desks).
3. If tagged, the mouse becomes a cat; if more than one is tagged, the first tagged becomes the cat.
4. If no one is tagged, the same child is the cat again. New children are chosen to be mice and the game begins again.

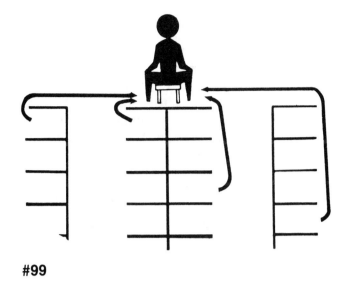

#99

101—Chain Tag
Playing Area: Playground with two parallel lines about 50' apart.
Players: 20 to 40
Equipment: None

1. A game involving goal exchange, all players except three stand behind a goal. Standing in the center of the two goals, the three remaining players form a chain by joining hands, using their free hands for tagging purposes.
2. On a signal from the three center players ("Come!"), the players behind the goal attempt to successfully run to the other goal without being tagged by the chain.
3. If tagged, those players become part of the chain, and the running from goal to goal begins again.
4. Should a chain become too long, the teacher may divide it into smaller chains.

100—Cat and Rat
Playing Area: Gym or playground
Players: 10 to 20
Equipment: None

1. All children except the cat and rat form a circle with hands joined.
2. The cat is outside the circle and the rat is inside.
3. The following conversation takes place:
   The cat: "I am the cat."
   The rat: "I am the rat."
   The cat: "I will catch you!"
   The rat: "No! You can't!"
4. The cat then chases the rat, attempting to tag him; but the circle protects the rat by letting him enter and leave the circle.
5. If he tags the rat, the cat becomes the rat and another child the cat.

102—Change Seats
Playing Area: Classroom
Players: Entire class
Equipment: None

1. With all children seated in their seats, the teacher commands, "Change left! Change right! Change front! Change back!" The children shift in the direction named, quickly and quietly.
2. If the shift is forward, those in the front row stand until commanded to "Change back!"
3. If the command is to shift right, those in the right-hand row of seats stand, and so on.

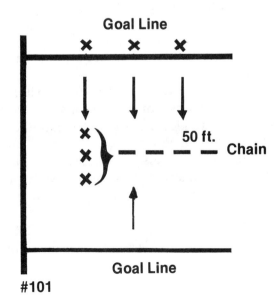

Goal Line

× × ×

↓ ↓ ↓

× **50 ft.**
× } - - - - - **Chain**
×

↑

Goal Line

#101

21

103—Chariot Relay

Playing Area: Gym or playground
Players: Entire class in groups of 3
Equipment: None

1. Two or more teams in file formation compete against each other in this relay game.
2. The chariot is formed by two players who grasp each other's hand as they stand side by side. A third player, the driver, stands behind the two and grasps the two outside hands of the chariot pair.
3. The three, in this formation and using a combination of the various locomotor movements, run from one goal to another and back, after which the next three players form their chariot.
4. The file to finish first wins the relay.

104—Charlie Over the Water

Playing Area: Gym or playground
Players: 15 to 20
Equipment: None

1. The players are in circle formation with hands joined. One player (Charlie) stands in the center of the circle.
2. The players, walking to either the left or right, chant:
   Charlie over the water,
   Charlie over the sea,
   Charlie caught a blackbird,
   But he can't catch me!
3. On "me" the players try to assume a squatting position before Charlie tags one of them.
4. If a player is tagged, he becomes the new Charlie in the center of the circle.

105—Circle Chase

Playing Area: Gym or playground
Players: 20 to 40
Equipment: None

1. The players, in circle formation, face the center; there should be plenty of space between players.
2. The children then count off by 3's, 4's or 5's.
3. When the teacher calls a number, the players with that number run in the same direction around the circle, attempting to tag the runner ahead and avoid being caught by the player behind.
4. Players who are caught drop out.
5. After all numbers have been called once, the remaining players count off again, and the game resumes until only a few remain.
6. Because those players tagged first are physically slow, the teacher should attempt to work them back into the game as soon as possible.

106—Circle Kick Ball

Playing Area: Gym or playground
Players: 10 to 20
Equipment: Soccer or rubber ball

1. The players form a circle, face inward, and join arms.
2. The ball is kicked back and forth within the circle (with the side of the foot) with each player attempting to kick the ball underneath the joined arms of two players.
3. If a player is successful in doing this, the two players who allowed the ball to leave the circle have a point scored against them or are eliminated from the game.
4. Should a player kick the ball over the arms of two players, a point is scored against the player who kicked the ball.

107—Circle Soccer

Playing Area: Gym
Players: 16-30 divided into two teams
Equipment: Soccer ball, slightly deflated

1. Players stand within the space of a double circle (20' and 18'), one team on each side of the center line.
2. The players on each team attempt to kick the ball through two players on the opposing team, below shoulder level.
3. Should a ball come to a dead stop within either half of the circle, a player in that half may throw the ball to a teammate; when a ball leaves the circle, it is put into play again at the point it left.
4. Players may use any part of their bodies, except hands and forearms, in blocking the ball from leaving the circle.
5. After each score, players move one place to the right.
6. A team can score a point if:
   a. a player on the opposing team touches the ball with his hands.
   b. it can kick the ball through the opposition.
   c. any player on the opposing team steps over the inner circle when he kicks.
   d. the ball is kicked higher than shoulder level by the opposing team.

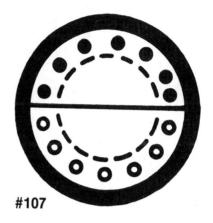

#107

108—Circle Stride Ball

Playing Area: Gym or playground
Players: 10 to 15 in circle formation
Equipment: Volleyball or rubber ball

1. Arranged in circle formation, the players take a stride position, with feet touching a foot of the player on each side. The hands are on the knees.
2. Standing in the center of the circle with the ball, the child who is "it" rolls the ball. He attempts to roll the ball between the feet of one of the players.
3. If successful, the person who allows the ball to leave the circle becomes "it," while the center player takes his place in the circle.
4. Players must use their hands to stop the ball and may not move their feet from the ground or floor.
5. If the ball goes between two players, the nearest one recovers it and play continues.

109—Circle Team Dodgeball

Playing Area: Gym or playground
Players: 20 to 40
Equipment: Volleyball or rubber ball

1. This game is played between two teams, one of which forms a circle and possesses the ball. The other team stands in the center of that circle.
2. At a signal, the circle players attempt to hit the center players below the shoulders.
3. Those center players hit may be eliminated; or a point may be scored for the circle players for each center player hit, with the center players remaining in the center.
4. A ball should not be held for more than one minute before being thrown.
5. After a designated playing time or until all center players have been hit, the two teams change positions.

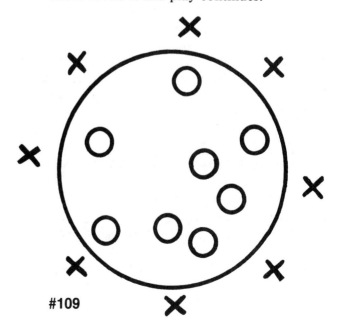

#109

110—Circle Tug-of-War

Playing Area: Gym or playground
Players: 10 to 15 in each circle
Equipment: 12 to 15 Indian clubs

1. Ten to fifteen players form a circle by joining hands in good strong grips and facing inward (however, it becomes more difficult to dodge the clubs when facing outward).
2. From ten to fifteen Indian clubs are placed in the center of the circle, scattered about its area.
3. Players attempt to force other players to either break grips or force a player to knock over a club by pushing and/or pulling.
4. Players (the pair) who do break grips or knock over a club are eliminated from the circle.
5. After the elimination, the circle is closed, and the tug-of-war continues until only three or four players remain. These players are declared the winners.

111—Circus Master

Playing Area: Gym or playground
Players: Any number
Equipment: None

1. A circle is formed, children facing inward, with one player, the "Circus Master," in the center, hand poised in imitation of a whip, ready to command the performances of the "animals."
2. The Circus Master has chosen an animal, the action of which the circle players are going to imitate; however, first he demonstrates the desired actions in the center of the circle.
3. After his demonstration and at his command, the children follow the imitation by moving around the circle, the Circus Master performing in the center.
4. At his signal, the children halt, the Circus Master becomes a circle player, and a new Circus Master is chosen.
5. All children should be given the opportunity to play Circus Master. It would be a good idea, also, if the children were instructed to secretly choose a particular animal to demonstrate prior to their being in the center.

112—Club Guard

Playing Area: Gym
Players: 8 to 10
Equipment: Indian club, volleyball or soccer ball

1. An 18" circle is drawn in the center of a 15' circle. An Indian club is placed in the 18" circle.
2. The circle players stand outside of the larger circle; a guard stands in the center of the larger circle but outside of the smaller circle.
3. Circle players throw the ball, attempting to knock over the club which the guard defends with any part of his body.
4. Circle players may pass the ball as rapidly as desired in an effort to find an unguarded opening.
5. The player who knocks over the club is the new guard.

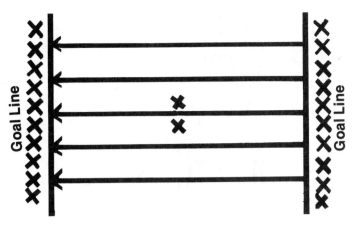

#113

114—Crossover

Playing Area: Playground with two parallel goal lines drawn 40' apart

Players: 15 to 20

Equipment: None

1. One child is chosen to be the catcher and stands in the center between two goal lines.
2. The remaining players are divided into two teams; each group stands behind one of the two goal lines.
3. The catcher faces one of the two teams and calls the name of one player from that team; that player in turn calls the name of a player on the opposite team.
4. With the catcher attempting to tag either one, the two players cross over and exchange goals while trying to avoid being tagged.
5. If one of the two players is tagged by the catcher, that player becomes the new catcher; the original catcher joins the team from which the tagged player is taken.

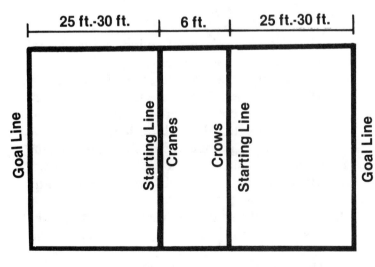

#115

113—Couples Tag

Playing Area: Gym, playground. Two goal lines are drawn 50' apart.

Players: Any number

Equipment: None

1. Children pair up with inside hands joined and line up behind one of two goal lines.
2. One couple stands in the center of the two goals and is "it."
3. At a signal from this center couple, the other couples behind the goal line run to the opposite goal keeping hands joined.
4. The center couple can only tag with their joined hands.
5. Couples caught help the center couple in tagging others. The game continues until all are caught. The last couple to be tagged is "it" for the next game.

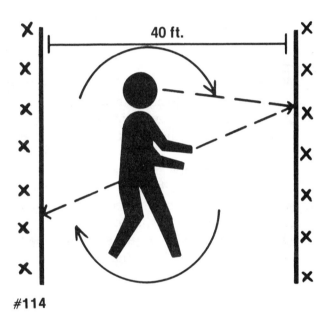

#114

115—Crows and Cranes

Playing Area: Playground, gym. Two goals are drawn about 56' apart.

Players: Any number

Equipment: None

1. Two teams, the crows and the cranes, face each other at the center of the area about 6' apart.
2. The teacher then gives the signal; if she calls "C-r-r-rows!" the crows run and are chased by the cranes.
3. If tagged by a crane before he reaches safety behind his own goal line, the crow becomes a crane.
4. On the signal, "C-r-r-ranes!" the cranes are chased by the crows.
5. The team with more players at the end of the playing period is the winner.

116—Do This, Do That

Playing Area: Playground, gym, classroom
Players: Entire class
Equipment: None

1. One child is chosen to lead the others in certain designated or spontaneous movements.
2. As the leader goes through these movements, he says, "Do This" or "Do That."
3. On "Do This," the other children must do as the leader is doing.
4. If the command is "Do That," no one should move; anyone who does move on this command is eliminated and must sit down in place.
5. The next leader is that child who is the last to remain standing.

117—Double Tag

Playing Area: Playground, gym. Two goal lines are drawn about 50' apart.
Players: Any number
Equipment: None

1. This game is similar to Couples Tag; players are paired with inside hands joined.
2. One pair of players with inside hands joined stands in the center between two goal lines. They attempt to tag couples as they run from one goal line to another; however, tagging may be done only with the joined hands of the "it" couple.
3. Any pairs of players tagged join the center couple and help in tagging others.
4. The last couple to be tagged or avoid being tagged is the "it" couple for the next game.

118—Dribble and Pivot Ball

Playing Area: Gym
Players: 4 to 8 on each team
Equipment: Basketball

1. Four to eight players in file formation form a team and stand behind a line.
2. The head player takes the ball, dribbles to a designated point, pivots so that he faces the line from which he started, and passes the ball to the next player in line, who goes through the same movements as the first player.
3. Each player, after completing the dribble, pivot, and pass, goes to the end of the file.

119—Dribble Call Ball

Playing Area: Gym
Players: 6 to 10 on each team
Equipment: Soccer balls

1. The players, in circle formation, are numbered consecutively in each circle-team.
2. A ball is placed in the center of each circle.
3. The teacher then calls a certain number; children in each circle possessing that number run to the center, pick up the ball, dribble it out the vacated spot, around the circle, back into the open spot, and into the center of the circle, where they place the ball by setting a foot lightly on it.
4. The first player to complete his round of the circle and return the ball to its center is the winner.
5. The game is resumed when a new number is called.

120—Eagle and Sparrows

Playing Area: Playground with two goal lines drawn 50' apart
Players: Entire class
Equipment: None

1. The Eagle sits in the center of a circle equidistant from the two parallel goal lines.
2. The other players or sparrows flutter around the eagle's nest.
3. Suddenly the Eagle rises from his nest and chases the sparrows to either one of the two goal lines.
4. Any sparrow caught joins the Eagle in his nest and helps catch the remaining sparrows.
5. Sparrows helping the Eagle may not run after untagged sparrows until the Eagle makes the first move.

122—Exchange Dodgeball

Playing Area: Playground or gym
Players: 12 to 20 in a circle formation
Equipment: Rubber ball

1. Players count off in such a fashion that two to four players within the circle have the same number.
2. One of the circle players is "it" and takes his position in the circle's center with a rubber ball at his feet.
3. When "it" calls a number, the players with that number run and exchange places. "It" picks up the ball and tries to hit one of the children.
4. If a circle player is hit below the waist by "it," the player hit now becomes "it;" if no circle player is hit, "it" remains in the center until successful.

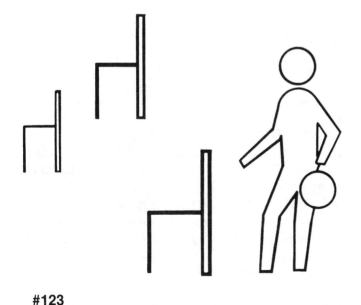

#123

121—End Ball

Playing Area: Gym
Players: Any number
Equipment: Basketball or rubber b

1. Approximately one-third of t team are end men; the remainde.
2. The game is started, with a toss up at the cen line. Each team's guards attempt to throw the ball to their end men.
3. A guard earns one point for a successful pass over the heads of the opposing team to his end men.
4. An end man, when he receives the ball, immediately throws it back to his guards; a guard man may keep or pass the ball in an attempt to score with a throw to his end men.
5. A ball which goes out of bounds is brought back inside the boundary at the point at which it went out and again put into play.
6. If a guard steps across the center line or into the opponent's end area, a foul is called and the ball is given to the nearest opponent.
7. The team with the greatest number of points within the playing time wins the game.

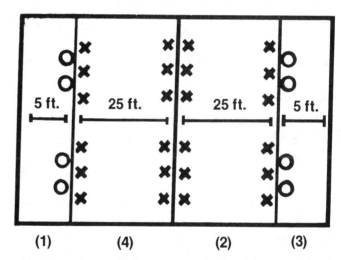

(1) End Men, Team A
(3) End Men, Team B
(2) Guards, Team A
(4) Guards, Team B
#121

123—Figure Eight Drill

Playing Area: Gym
Players: 4 to 8 in file formation
Equipment: Basketball, 3 objects which represent opponents

1. The players dribble the ball around the objects and then shoot the ball.
2. Their bodies must always be between the object and the basketball, so they must change hands for this purpose.
3. Players should practice shooting while standing still or in motion.

...owers and Wind

...g Area: Playground, gym. Two parallel lines
...drawn 30' apart.
...ayers: 10 to 30
Equipment: None

1. The players are divided into two groups.
    a. The flowers secretly select the name of a flower.
    b. The wind guesses the name of the flower selected.
2. The flowers walk to within 3' of the wind's goal line.
3. When the wind guesses the name of the flower, those players chase the flowers, trying to tag them before they reach their goal line.
4. Any players who are caught join the group called the wind.

#125

126—Four Square

Playing Area: Gym or blacktop surface
Players: 4 at a time
Equipment: Volleyball or rubber ball

1. The object of the game is to advance to quadrant A and stay there as long as possible.
2. The rotation of players is from D to C to B and finally to A.
3. Player D starts the game by bounce serving the ball to any one of the other players. If unsuccessful, he goes out of the game.
4. The player to whom the ball was served returns the ball to any of the other three squares after one bounce.
5. Play continues until a player commits one of the following violations:
    a. The ball lands on a line or out of the court area.
    b. The ball is hit with the fist.
    c. The ball hits a player in another quadrant; the player who is hit goes down.
    d. A player momentarily holds the ball.
6. When a violation occurs, the violator goes down to D; the other players move up in regular rotation. When D is the violator, he is out of the game. The first player in waiting line becomes D.

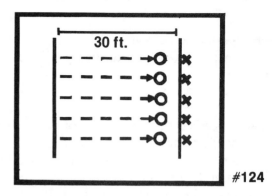

#124

125—Fly Trap

Playing Area: Playground, gym
Players: Entire class
Equipment: None

1. The players are divided into two groups:
    a. One group, the Traps, sit Indian-fashion spread around the room.
    b. The other group, the Flies, buzz around the Traps.
2. When the signal is given, the Flies freeze at the spot.
3. If a Trap can reach one of the Flies, the Fly must sit down and become a Trap.
4. The game ends when all the Flies are caught.

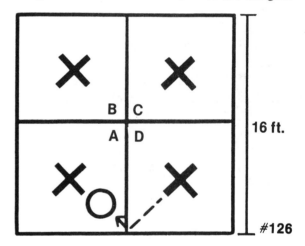

#126

127—Four-Team Grab Ball

Playing Area: Playground, gym
Players: Four teams, 6 to 8 on each
Equipment: 4 balls of same size but different colors

1. The players are divided into groups of four.
2. A line is drawn 30' to 50' from a wall.
3. Players line up behind each other. The head players stand behind the line and throw the balls against the wall.
4. These players then try to get another team's ball and return to the original starting position.
5. First player to accomplish this scores 2 points for his team, second player scores 1, third and fourth score nothing. If a player returns his own ball, his team loses a point.
6. These players go to the end of the line and the next four players try their luck.

28

128—Fourth Down

Playing Area: One-half of a football field
Players: Two teams, 6 to 12 on each team
Equipment: Football

1. Each play is a fourth down so the offensive team must score in one play.
2. The offense can pass from behind or beyond the line of scrimmage.
3. The first offensive player to receive the ball from center cannot be tagged for ten seconds unless he runs with the ball.
4. Defensive players must stay ten feet from this man.
5. A two-handed tag above the waist is required to down a runner or pass-receiver.
6. If the pass is incomplete, the defense takes over at the original line of scrimmage.

129—Freeze Tag

Playing Area: Playground, gym
Players: Entire class
Equipment: None

1. One child is "it" while the other players run around trying not to be touched.
2. When the person who is "it" approaches a child, he must remain completely motionless to be safe.
3. If he is tagged before he can freeze, he becomes the person who is "it."

130—Frog in the Sea

Playing Area: A small area indoors or outdoors
Players: 6 to 8 in each game
Equipment: None

1. The child selected to be the Frog sits cross-legged in the center of a circle.
2. The other players call, "Frog in the sea, can't catch me!" while stepping in and out of the circle daring the frog to catch them.
3. The frog tries to tag someone without leaving his sitting position.
4. Anyone whom he tags changes places with him and the game continues.

131—Gallop Tag

Playing Area: Playground, gym
Players: 12 to 20
Equipment: None

1. The players stand in a circle formation, facing in.
2. The player who is "it" walks around the outside of the circle and tags another player on the back.
3. "It" then gallops around the circle while the other player chases him.
4. If he reaches the vacated spot without being tagged, the other person is then "it"; otherwise he must try again with another player.

132—Hill Dill

Playing Area: Playground. Two parallel lines are drawn 50' apart.
Players: 10 to 50
Equipment: None

1. The child who is "it" stands in the center of the play area.
2. The other players, divided in two equal groups, stand behind one of the goal lines marked across the ends of the play area.
3. The child who is "it" calls, "Hill Dill! Come over the hill!"
4. On this signal, the players run across the center space to the opposite goals while the child who is "it" tries to tag them.
5. The tagged players go to the center and help tag the remaining players.
6. The game continues until all players are tagged.

133—Hindoo Freeze
Playing Area: Gym or playground
Players: Entire class
Equipment: None
1. The players are scattered over a limited playing area.
2. One is chosen as "it" and attempts to tag another player.
3. The players are safe when in a motionless "Hindoo" position, that is, on their knees with the forehead resting on the hands on the floor.

134—Home Run
Playing Area: Softball diamond. First base and home plate are used.
Players: 4 to 10
Equipment: Softball, bat
1. A pitcher, catcher, batter, and fielder are the selected players. Other players are fielders.
2. The ball is pitched. If the batter hits a fair ball, he runs to first base and back home before the ball is returned to the catcher.
3. Batter is out in the event of the following:
    a. A fly ball or fair ball is caught.
    b. He strikes out.
    c. He does not return to home before the ball reaches the catcher.
4. The distance between home plate and first base should depend on the ability of the players.

135—Hook On
Playing Area: Playground, gym
Players: 15 to 30
Equipment: None
1. The players are scattered in twos over a limited playing area.
2. One is chosen as a chaser and the other as a runner.
3. The players join inside hands and place outside hands on hips making a hook for the runner to latch on to.
4. When the chaser tags the runner, the runner becomes the chaser.
5. The runner is safe if he can hook on to a pair of the other players.
6. The outside player of this trio then becomes the runner.

136—Hound and Rabbit
Playing Area: Playground, gym
Players: 15 to 30
Equipment: None
1. One child is the Rabbit and stands outside the Trees.
2. The Trees are formed by two children facing forward and holding hands with a Rabbit in the center.
3. A Hound chases the extra Rabbit who takes refuge in any one of the Trees.
4. Only one Rabbit is allowed in a tree at a time, so the other Rabbit is then forced out of the Tree and chased by the Hound until he finds a Tree.
5. The Rabbit who is caught by the Hound becomes the new Hound.

137—Individual Dodgeball
Playing Area: Playground, gym
Players: Two teams, 10 to 15 on each
Equipment: 2 volleyballs
1. Two teams of the same number form circles of the same size.
2. A player from each team stands inside the opponent's circle.
3. The players in the circle aim the ball at the player inside the circle.
4. The team which hits the inner player first gains a point.

138—In The Creek
Playing Area: Playground, gym, classroom
Players: Entire class
Equipment: None
1. Two lines are drawn 2' to 3' apart to represent the banks of the creek.
2. All the children face the creek lined up on one of the banks.
3. If the leader says "In the creek," the children jump into the creek; if the leader says, "On the bank," the children jump to the other bank.
4. If a wrong move is made or if the children jump out of place or step over a line, they are out of the game.

139—Jump the Shot

Playing Area: Playground, gym
Players: 10 to 20
Equipment: A jump-the-shot rope

1. Players stand in a circle facing the center.
2. The player holding the rope kneels in the center of the circle and turns the rope, playing it out to its full length until sufficient momentum keeps the **weighted end** of it turning under the feet of the players in the circle, who must jump over it.
3. Any player who touches the rope with his feet while it is turning is "out," and he leaves the circle.
4. The last player "out" turns the rope for the repetition of the game.

140—Keep Away

Playing Area: Football field or large play space
Players: Two teams, 8 to 12 on each side
Equipment: Football, pinnies or colored shirts

1. Two teams each with six to eight players are scattered over the play area.
2. A ball is tossed into the area.
3. Players attempt to recover the ball and pass it among their own team members while the opponents attempt to intercept the passes.
4. If two opponents catch a pass at the same time, the teacher tosses the ball between them, and they try to bat the ball to their own team members; they cannot catch the ball on the toss-up.

141—Keep It Up

Playing Area: Playground, gym
Players: 5 to 8 players on each team
Equipment: Volleyballs

1. Each team forms a small circle.
2. Upon a signal, the team's ball is tossed into play by a team member.
3. The players attempt to keep their team's ball in the air by batting it with open hands, and the team which keeps its ball up the longest wins a point.
4. The team which earns the most points within the playing period wins.

142—Kick Over

Playing Area: Football field with a ten-yard end zone
Players: 6 to 10 on each team
Equipment: Football

1. Players form two equal teams with each team scattered on opposite ends of the field.
2. The object of the game is to kick the ball over the end zone of the opponent from 20 to 30 feet in front of the goal line.
3. If the opponent catches the ball inside the end zone, no score is made; if the ball is not caught, a goal is scored.
4. If the ball is caught, it is kicked 3 strides from the place where it is caught.
5. If the ball is not caught, it is kicked from the place where it landed.

143—Kick Pin Softball

Playing Area: Softball diamond. See diagram.

Players: Two teams, 8 to 12 on a side

Equipment: 1 soccer ball, 4 Indian clubs placed on outside corner of each base and on home plate

1. Players form two equal teams with a catcher, pitcher, three basemen and fielders on each.
2. The "batter" kicks the ball rolled by the pitcher and runs around the outside of the bases until he reaches home plate.
3. While he is running, a fielder recovers the ball and throws it successfully to first, second, third and then home. Each baseman kicks over the club and passes the ball on to the next base.
4. A point is scored only if the "batter" reaches home plate before the ball does.
5. The "batter" is out if:
   a. The club is knocked over by the pitcher at home plate.
   b. The second ball is a foul ball.
   c. The "batter" kicks the ball and knocks over one of the clubs.
   d. A fly ball is caught by a fielder.
   e. The ball is caught and the club knocked over by a baseman before the "batter" reaches that base.

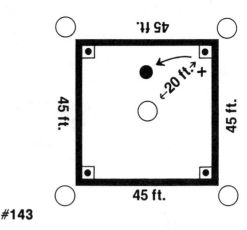

#143

144—Lane and Shuttle Relay

Playing Area: Playground, gym

Players: Two teams, 4 to 8 on each

Equipment: None

1. Players on each team line up behind the starting line.
2. A special movement, such as hopping, skipping or jumping is designated.
3. When the signal is given, the first player in each file runs to the goal, returns to the starting line, tags the second player, and goes to the end of the line.
4. Each player, in turn, is tagged, runs, tags the next player, and takes his place at the end of the file.
5. The team wins which finishes first with all of the players back in their original places in the file, provided no fouls have been made by the team. It is a foul for a player to start before he is tagged or to fail to observe a rule.
6. Variations are made by having the children imitate objects or animals in the relay.

145—Last Couple Out

Playing Area: Playground, gym

Players: 10 to 15

Equipment: None

1. The players are in couples in a double file formation.
2. The player who is "it" stands from 3 to 5 feet in front of the first couple in the file, with his back toward the other players.
3. He calls "Last couple out!" The two players of the last couple separate and run forward on the outside of the file and attempt to catch hands in front of "it" before either is tagged.
4. The child who is "it" cannot turn around.
5. The player whom he tags becomes his partner and the other is "it"; if he tags no one, he is "it" again.
6. The couple goes to the head of the file and a new couple is the "last couple" for the repetition of the game.

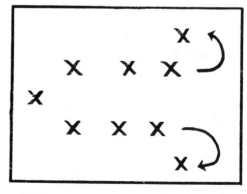

#145

146—Lay-Up Drill

Playing Area: Basketball court
Players: Any number
Equipment: Basketball

1. The first player in one file passes the ball to the first player in the other file, who advances toward the basket for a lay-up shot.
2. Each player goes to the end of the opposite file after each play.

147—Leaping the Brook

Playing Area: Playground, gym
Players: Entire class
Equipment: None

1. Two lines are drawn to represent the banks of the brook.
2. The children run and jump over the brook.
3. Anyone missing the jump and landing in the brook is sent "home" to put on dry shoes and socks. He goes "home," pretends to take off his shoes and socks, puts them back on, and then re-enters the game.

148—Line Soccer

Playing Area: Soccer field. Two goal lines 50' to 80' apart with sidelines 40' to 60' wide
Players: 10 to 20 on each team
Equipment: Soccer ball

1. The play space is divided into three equal areas: one central and two ends.
2. The object of the game is to kick the ball over the opponent's rear boundary line.
3. On the signal to start play, the referee drops the ball in the central area, and one player from each team runs to the center and tries to kick the ball.
4. A ball which goes out of bounds is recovered by the opponents of the team which last touched the ball.
5. After the players become skillful, the game may be scored.
6. One point is scored for each ball kicked over the opponent's rear boundary line.

149—Locomotive Tag

Playing Area: Playground, gym
Players: Entire class
Equipment: None

1. The players are scattered over the play area.
2. The child who is "it" tells the other children how to move, i.e., jump, hop, slide, or run. "It" must do the same motions.
3. The player whom he tags becomes "it."

150—Loop Touch

Playing Area: Playground, gym. Three parallel lines are drawn 15' apart.
Players: Any number divided in pairs
Equipment: None

1. The players are divided into pairs, standing facing each other on the end lines.
2. When the signal is given, the partners run to the center lines, join right hands, run around each other (right-hand loop) and return to their starting line.
3. Without stopping, they run to their partners, make the left loop and return.
4. They repeat with the two-hand loop..
5. The first pair to return to the starting line after all stunts have been performed wins the game.

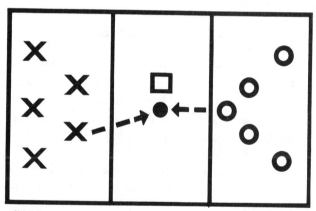

#148

151—Lost Children

Playing Area: Classroom
Players: Entire class
Equipment: None

1. The child who is "it" leaves the room.
2. While he is gone, the rest of the children leave their seats and walk around the room.
3. When "it" returns the teacher says, "The children are lost. Please, lead them safely home."
4. "It" then tries to seat the children in their own places; the object is to see how many he can seat accurately.

152—March Attack

Playing Area: Playground, gym. Two parallel lines are drawn 60' apart.
Players: Two teams, 15 to 20 on each
Equipment: None

1. A definite space at one end of the play area is the chasers' home.
2. The other team standing on a line opposite the chasers is the marching team.
3. When the signal is given, the marchers begin marching across to the line of the chasers, who have their backs to them.
4. Another signal is given and the chasers turn around and try to catch the marchers before they can reach their line.
5. If a marcher is tagged by a chaser, he becomes a chaser and assists in tagging the other marchers in their next venture forth.

155—Modified Soccer

Playing Area: 100' x 150' area
Players: 7 on each team
Equipment: Soccer pinnies, soccer ball

1. Each team selects a goalie and the rest of the players are divided into forwards and guards.
2. Each team has a goal at the end of the boundary line approximately 24 feet wide.
3. The object of the game is to kick the ball over the opponent's rear goal line.
4. A coin is tossed to determine who kicks off.
5. If a ball goes over the end line other than over the goal line, two different free kicks are enacted.
   a. If the opponents last touched the ball, the goalie takes a free kick by setting the ball down in front of the goal and trying to kick the ball over the goal line.
   b. If the defenders last touched the ball, a forward kicks the ball over the goal line on a free kick.
6. One point is scored for each ball kicked over the opponent's rear goal line, whether it be on a free kick or during regular playing time.

153—Midnight

Playing Area: Playground
Players: 6 to 15
Equipment: None

1. One child is chosen to be the fox, who stands in his den.
2. The other players ask, "What time is it?" and move slowly to the fox's den.
3. The fox answers the question as the children keep coming closer and closer.
4. When he answers the question with "Midnight," the children try to run back to their line of safety without being caught by the fox.
5. Any child who is tagged must join the fox in the den and help him capture the rest of the players.

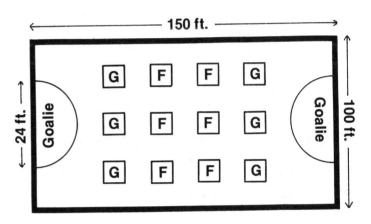

#155

156—Mousetrap

Playing Area: Playground, gym, classroom
Players: 20 to 40
Equipment: None

1. The children are divided into two equal teams.
2. One team, the Mousetraps, joins hands in a circle formation, facing the middle.
3. The other team, the Mice, is scattered around outside the circle.
4. When a signal is given, the Traps open and the Mice run in and out of the circle between the Traps.
5. Another signal is given, and the Traps snap shut (arms come down).
6. All mice caught join the Traps and try to capture the remaining Mice.

157—Newcomb

Playing Area: Volleyball court
Players: Two teams, 8 to 10 on each
Equipment: Volleyball

1. Each team occupies one side of the court.
2. Play is started with a player on one team throwing the ball into the opposite court.
3. The players throw the ball back and forth over the net attempting to hit the floor of the opponent's court with the ball.
4. A point is made if the ball thrown over the net hits the floor of the opponent's court provided the ball does not touch the net going over.
5. A ball going outside the boundary lines is recovered by the nearest player, who brings it into the court at the point it went out and puts it into play.

158—Nose and Toe Tag

Playing Area: Playground, gym
Players: Entire class
Equipment: None

1. The players are scattered over the play area.
2. The child who is "it" tries to tag another player.
3. A player may escape being tagged by grasping his nose with one hand and his foot with the other hand.
4. A player who is tagged becomes "it" and the game continues.

159—O'Grady Says

Playing Area: Classroom
Players: Entire class
Equipment: None

1. One player is selected as the leader.
2. He stands in front of the room and the other players stand in the aisles facing the leader.
3. The leader gives commands, some of which are prefaced by "O'Grady says" and some of which are not.
4. Any player who makes a mistake by not doing a command preceded by "O'Grady says" or by doing a command not preceded by "O'Grady says" must sit down in his seat if the leader sees the error and calls his name.
5. After the leader has caught three players making errors, another leader is selected.

160—One-Bounce Volleyball

Playing Area: Volleyball court
Players: Two teams, 6 to 9 each
Equipment: Volleyball

1. Each team is scattered over one of two courts separated by a net.
2. Side and end boundary lines enclose the courts.
3. Play is started by a player on one team, chosen by chance.
4. The players bat the ball back and forth over the net.
5. A point is made if the ball batted over the net hits the floor of the opponent's court and bounces more than once before it is returned to the other court.
6. Any ball going outside the boundary lines is recovered by the nearest player, who brings it into the court at the point where it went out and puts it into play.

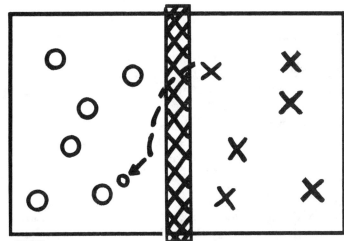

#160

161—One, Two, Button My Shoe

Playing Area: Playground, gym. Two parallel lines are drawn 50' apart.
Players: Entire class
Equipment: None

1. One child is the leader and stands to one side of the play area.
2. The remaining players are lined up on one of the goal lines.
3. A riddle is chanted by the leader and the other players:

Children	Leader's Response
One, two	Button my shoe.
Three, four	Close the door.
Five, six	Pick up sticks.
Seven, eight	Run, or you'll be **late!**

4. When the leader says "late," that is the signal for the children to run to the other line and back. The first one back becomes the new leader.

162—Over and Under Relay

Playing Area: Gym, playground
Players: Entire class in file formation
Equipment: Ball for each file

1. Players are in a file formation behind a starting line.
2. The first player in each file has a ball.
3. At the signal to start, the first player passes the ball over his head to the second player, who passes it between his legs to the third.
4. The ball is passed "over and under" the whole length of the file.
5. The last player, upon receiving the ball, runs forward to the front of his file and starts the ball again.
6. This is continued until the file is back in its original lineup with the ball in the hands of the original first player.
7. The file finishing first wins.

164—Poison Circle

Playing Area: Playground, gym
Players: 8 to 12 in each circle
Equipment: Volleyball or rubber ball

1. The players are in a circle formation with hands joined.
2. Another circle is drawn two feet inside this circle with a ball in the center of it.
3. The players try to pull or push another player into the center circle without crossing the line of the center circle.
4. When a player crosses the line of the center circle, he picks up the ball in the center and tries to hit someone below the waist with it.
5. If he hits someone, this player has a black mark scored against him; if he misses, the thrower has a black mark against him.
6. The first person to have three black marks scored against him must pay a penalty.

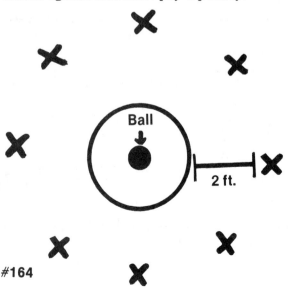

#164

163—Pass and Squat Relay

Playing Area: Gym, playground
Players: Entire class in file formation with the leader about 10' in front of his team
Equipment: Ball for each file

1. The relay starts on a signal and the ball is tossed from the leader to the player in first position who tosses the ball back to leader and then squats down.
2. The leader then passes the ball to the next in line who tosses it back to the leader and squats, and the game continues the same way until the last in line catches the ball.
3. When the player at the end of the line receives the ball, he runs with the ball to the leader's position; the former leader runs to the position at the head of the line, and the relay is over.

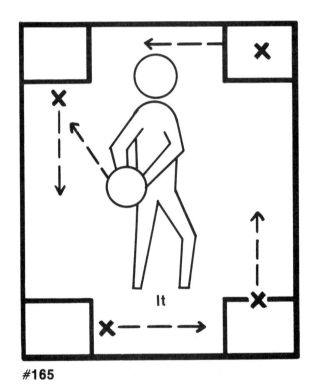

#165

165—Poor Puppy

Playing Area: Gym with designated "corners"
Players: 8 to 10
Equipment: Large rubber ball

1. Each player has a "corner" or definite goal.
2. The player who is "it" has no corner and tries to get a goal by tagging another player with the ball.
3. He tags a player by hitting him below the waist with the ball when the player is not on a goal.
4. All players change corners when "it" calls, "Poor Puppy. Puppy wants a corner!"
5. When a player is tagged fairly, he becomes "it" and the game continues.

166—Prisoner's Base

Playing Area: Rectangular area. See diagram.
Players: Two teams with 5 to 15 on each side
Equipment: None

1. Two teams are formed and each is assigned to one of two bases which are marked at opposite ends of the play area.
2. Each team has a prison near its base.
3. The players try to take all of the opponents as prisoners.
4. Any player may be tagged only by an opponent who has left his own base after the player who is tagged.
5. Safety is attained by a player who has left his base by capturing an opponent, freeing a prisoner, or returning to his base before he is tagged.
6. A player who has tagged an opponent fairly can take his captive to prison without being tagged.
7. A prisoner can be freed by being tagged by a member of his team who has reached him in prison without getting caught, and both may then return to their base safely.
8. Players may return to their bases at any time, and then they are free to tag any opponent who is out when they leave their base again.

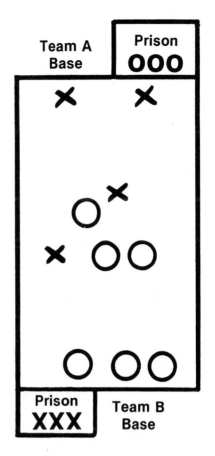

#166

168—Right Face, Left Face

Playing Area: Playground, gym
Players: 25 to 35
Equipment: None

1. The players are arranged in several lines containing an equal number of players.
2. When the players face the front of the room and join hands, the aisles which form between the lines are in a right face position.
3. When they face the side of the room and join hands, the aisles are in a left face positon.
4. There are two extra players, one who is "it" and one who is the runner.
5. "It" chases the runner through the aisles formed by the players.
6. These aisles are changed when the leader calls "right face" or "left face."
7. When "right face" is called, all quickly face the front and join hands; when "left face" is called, all quickly face the side and join hands again.
8. Changing the aisles may either assist or hinder "it" in tagging the runner.
9. When the runner is tagged, a new runner and chaser are selected and the original two players take their places in the lines of participants.

167—Roll Dodgeball

Playing Area: Playground, gym
Players: Two teams, 20 to 30 on each
Equipment: 2 volleyballs or rubber balls

1. One team forms a circle; the other team is inside the circle.
2. The circle players roll the balls at the feet of the center players, trying to hit them.
3. When a center player is hit, he leaves the circle.
4. The last one remaining in the center wins the game.
5. The teams then trade places.

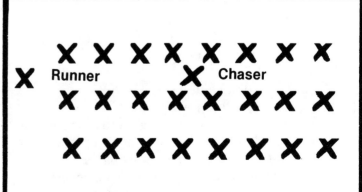

#168

37

169—Red Light

Playing Area: 60' to 100' across with goal line
Players: Entire class
Equipment: None

1. The player selected to be "it" stands on a goal line marked across one end of the play area.
2. The other players are on a starting line at the opposite end.
3. The child who is "it" calls, "Green light!"
4. He turns his back to the players and counts from one to ten and adds, "Red light!"
5. The players start on the signal, "Green light!" and run toward the goal line, but they must stop on the words, "Red light!"
6. On this signal, "it" turns to face the players.
7. If he sees a player moving his feet, he sends him back to the starting line.
8. Each player tries to be the first to reach the goal line.
9. The game continues until all are over the goal line.
10. The last player over the line is "it" as the game is repeated.

170—Running Dodgeball

Playing Area: Playground, gym. Area is 40' by 60'
Players: Two teams, 10 to 15 on each team
Equipment: 4 volleyballs

1. Half of Team A's players are behind a goal line marked across one end of the play area.
2. The other half of Team A is on the other goal line marked at the opposite end.
3. Team B tries to run between the aisles formed by the first team without being touched by balls, while Team A throws the balls at their feet trying to hit them.
4. A ball that has stopped inside or outside the play area must be brought back to one of the starting lines before it can be thrown again.
5. When a player is out, he leaves the play area for the time remaining in that playing period.

171—Scrub (Work-Up)

Playing Area: Softball field
Players: 7 to 15
Equipment: Softball and bat

1. Each player plays for himself.
2. When the batter is out, he goes to a position in right field. All other players move up one position with the catcher becoming batter.
3. If the batted ball falls behind the home line, it is a foul ball; the batter cannot run on a foul ball.
4. If he bats a fair ball he runs to first base and back to the home plate.

5. One point is scored if he returns to the home plate without being put "out." He is put out if:
   a. An opponent catches his batted ball before it hits the ground.
   b. An opponent tags him with the ball.
   c. An opponent throws the ball to the catcher before the batter reaches home plate.
6. Each player plays an equal number of turns in the field and at bat.
7. The player who has made the most points during the playing time wins the game.

172—Set Shot Formation
Playing Area: Basketball court
Players: 6 to 8
Equipment: None
1. The leader stands aside from the other players who are in a semicircle facing the basket.
2. The leader throws the ball to each player in order; this player shoots the ball toward the basket trying to score a point.
3. After each player has had an attempt at shooting, he backs up and shoots again.
4. Each player should have a turn as leader.
5. At the end of the playing period, the player with the highest score wins the game.

174—Simon Says
Playing Area: Classroom
Players: Entire class
Equipment: None
1. One player is selected as the leader.
2. He stands in the front of the room and the other players stand in the aisles facing the leader.
3. The leader gives commands; some are prefaced by "Simon says" and some are not.
4. The players must do everything commanded which is preceded by "Simon says"; they must not obey a command which is not preceded by "Simon says."
5. Any player who makes a mistake must sit down in his seat if the leader sees the error and calls his name.
6. After the leader has caught three players making errors, another leader is selected.
7. The three players get into the game again.
8. The game starts again with the new leader giving the commands.

176—Stoop Tag
Playing Area: Playground, gym
Players: Entire class
Equipment: None
1. The players are scattered over the play area.
2. The child who is "it" tries to tag another player.
3. A player may escape being tagged by touching both hands to the ground in a stooped position.
4. A player who is tagged becomes "it" and the game is continued.

173—Sideline Basketball
Playing Area: Basketball court
Players: Class divided into two teams
Equipment: Basketball
1. Two teams are chosen with an equal number of players on each team.
2. Half the players on each team are active players and the other players stand outside the playing area.
3. Regular basketball rules are enforced, except that when a ball lands out of bounds, a sideline player recovers the ball and passes it to one of the active players on his team.
4. When a signal is given, the sideline players become the active players, and the active players become the sideline players.
5. The team which scores the greater number of points at the end of the playing period wins the game.

175—Squirrel in the Trees
Playing Area: Playground, gym
Players: 15 to 35
Equipment: None
1. A tree is formed by two players joining hands. The squirrel is in the center of each tree. Extra squirrels are outside.
2. The groups of three are scattered over the play area.
3. The teacher calls, "Squirrels run!"
4. This is the signal for the squirrels to run from their tree to another tree; while they are changing to another tree the extra squirrels attempt to get into a tree.
5. Only one squirrel is allowed in a tree and someone is always left without a tree.
6. As soon as all of the trees are full, the signal is repeated and the game continues.

177—Stop and Start
Playing Area: Playground, gym
Players: Entire class
Equipment: None
1. The players stand behind one of two goal lines; a leader stands off to the side, out of the path of the players.
2. The leader gives a command which utilizes the various locomotor skills the children have learned; on this command the children execute the desired movement. ("Leap!")
3. When the leader yells "Stop," all players must come to an immediate halt in place; any player caught moving is sent back to the starting line.
4. The first player to reach the opposite goal is the winner and new leader.

178—Stride Bowling

Playing Area: Playground, gym
Players: 4 to 6
Equipment: Volleyball or rubber ball

1. One player is the target, and he stands with legs spread apart in stride position. Another player stands somewhat behind the target and is the catcher.
2. The remaining players stand behind a foul line some fifteen to twenty feet away from the target.
3. Each takes a turn at bowling the ball through the legs of the target. Two chances are allowed each player. Two points are scored for rolling the ball through the legs of the target, and one point for hitting the leg of the target.

179—Tag

Playing Area: Playground, gym
Players: Any number
Equipment: None

1. The simplest game of tag is played by scattering children over the playing area and designating one child to be "it."
2. The children run, trying to avoid being tagged by "it;" "it" chases and attempts to tag one of the running players; if successful in tagging a player, this player is the new "it."
3. Children may be safe by:
   a. touching a previously designated goal, object, or color.
   b. assuming a certain position or pose (See specific tag games.)

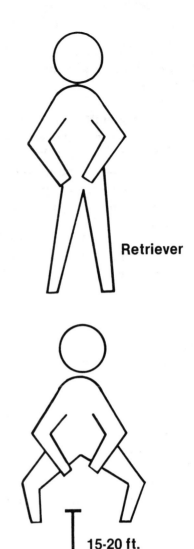

Retriever

15-20 ft.

#178

Players Behind Foul Line

180—Teacher Ball

Playing Area: Playground, gym
Players: 6 to 8
Equipment: Volleyball or rubber ball

1. Children line up facing a designated leader or teacher.
2. Beginning with the person on his left, the leader throws the ball to each child in one line; each child must catch the ball and return it to the leader.
3. Any player in the line who fails to catch or throw the ball correctly goes to the end of the line (to the leader's right) and each player then moves up one space.
4. The leader attempts to successfully complete three successive rounds of throwing and catching without an error. If he does so, he scores a point for himself, goes to the end of the line, and the head player becomes the new teacher or leader. If the leader does err, he goes to the end of the line and the head player becomes the new leader.

181—Ten, Ten, Double Ten

Playing Area: Classroom
Players: Entire class
Equipment: Small object

1. This game involves placing a small object in an inconspicuous place in the classroom. This is done by one child while the rest of the class leaves the room.
2. When the children return to the room, they begin their search. The first child to spot the object remains silent until he reaches his seat; he then calls, "Ten, ten, double ten, forty-five, fifteen, buckskin six," and sits down.
3. The game is then begun again. The object is placed, as before, in an inconspicuous place in the classroom by the child who was first to spot the object in the previous game.

182—The Hunter

Playing Area: Playground, gym, classroom
Players: Entire class
Equipment: Marker or seat for each child

1. One child is chosen to be the leader or the Hunter.
2. Walking around the room or playing area, the Hunter calls, "Who wants to hunt . . .?" (Any animal may be chosen.) Those players who choose to hunt follow behind the Hunter.
3. At any time he wishes, the Hunter yells, "Bang!" This is the signal for those following the Hunter to return to their markers or seats.
4. The first player to return is the Hunter for the next game.

183—Three Deep

Playing Area: Playground, gym
Players: 20 to 30
Equipment: None

1. A runner and a chaser are chosen. The remaining children form a double circle (player behind player, all facing inward, two deep).
2. Within the immediate inside and outside area of the circle, the chaser pursues the runner and attempts to tag him. The runner escapes by taking a position directly in front of any two players, thus forming a three-deep combination. The last of the three players now becomes the runner, and he may escape in the same manner as the first runner.
3. If the chaser succeeds in tagging the runner, their roles are reversed.

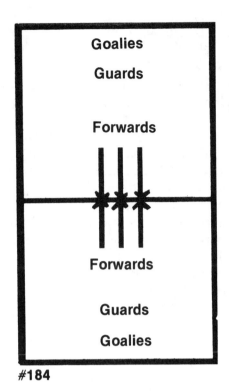

#184

184—Three-Line Soccer

Playing Area: Soccer field. See diagram.
Players: 15 to 20 on each team
Equipment: Soccer ball

1. For the general rules of Three-Line Soccer, see Line Soccer, #148.
2. The two opposing teams are each divided into three equal sections—forwards, guards, goalies.
3. The game begins with a kickoff at the center line. After the opening kick, successive kicks are made by the team which failed to score. After a score, teams rotate playing positions.
4. Although goalies may use their hands in defending the goal, other players must abide by soccer rules. If a guard or forward touches the ball with his hands, he scores a foul against his team and the opposing team wins a free kick.

185—Through the Tunnel Race

Playing Area: Playground, gym, classroom
Players: 6 to 8 on each team
Equipment: None

1. Teams compete against each other in relay formation. Each team lines up back to back and stands with their legs apart.
2. The end player of the relay crawls through the spread legs of his teammates. When he reaches the front of his file, he takes the front position and the next player crawls through, and so on until the relay team members are again in their starting positions.
3. The first team to reach its original position is the winner.

#185

186—Throw It and Run Softball

Playing Area: Softball field reduced in size
Players: Two teams of 9 players
Equipment: Softball

1. This game is played very much similar to the game of softball.
2. There are three exceptions:
   a. When the pitcher throws the ball, the batter catches the ball and throws it into the outfield. Once the ball enters the outfield, it is treated just as a batted ball is in softball.
   b. If the batter throws a foul ball, it counts as an out for the batter and his team; each team is allowed three outs.
   c. No stealing is allowed during the course of a batter's progress from base to base; the runner must remain on base until the batter has thrown the ball.

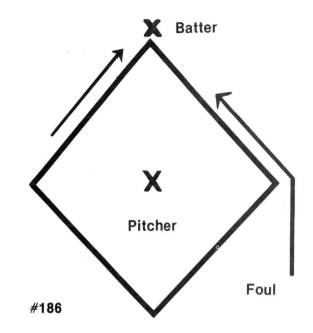

#186

187—Weathervane

Playing Area: Classroom
Players: Entire class
Equipment: None

1. The children are standing next to their seats.
2. The teacher gives the command: "North," "South," "East," or "West."
3. At the command, the children shift in the direction named.
4. When the shift is in the direction they are facing, they continue to play in a standing position until the next command is given.
5. If a child makes more than one error, he must sit down in his seat.

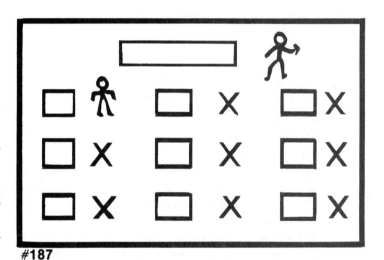

#187

188—Where, Oh Where

Playing Area: Classroom
Players: Entire class
Equipment: Small object that can be hidden in a child's hand

1. One child is selected to be "it" and turns his back to the class while hiding his eyes.
2. The children are sitting at their desks.
3. A small article is passed from child to child until "it" says, "Where, Oh Where?"
4. "It" turns around and tries to guess in three guesses who has the object in his hand.
5. If he guesses, the child with the object becomes "it." If not, "it" tries again.

#188

43

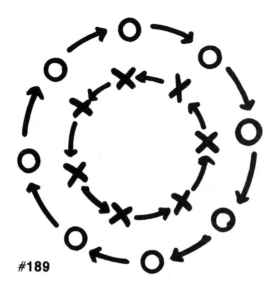

#189

189—Where's My Partner

Playing Area: Playground, gym
Players: Entire class
Equipment: None

1. The players are arranged in couples.
2. Partners stand facing each other, forming two circles.
3. One extra player in the outside circle does not have a partner.
4. Upon a signal from the teacher, the outside players walk around the circle clockwise, while the inside circle players walk around counterclockwise.
5. When the teacher says, "Stop!" the players stop walking and each attempts to get a partner.
6. The player without a partner is in the "Mush Pot."

190—Wiggle Worm Race

Playing Area: Playground, gym
Players: Entire class
Equipment: None

1. Teams are in a relay formation.
2. Each player places his right hand through his legs into the left hand of the player behind him.
3. At the signal, the whole file moves to the goal and back.
4. The team wins which finishes the relay first, provided they kept their hands clasped.

#190

191—Work-Up

Playing Area: Softball field
Players: 4 to 10 players on each team
Equipment: Softball and bat

1. The four necessary players are the pitcher, catcher, batter, and one fielder.
2. The other players are fielders.
3. Each player scores for himself when he is the batter.
4. The batter scores by hitting a fair ball and running to first base and back to home plate before the ball can be returned to the catcher.
5. The batter is out when:
   a. A fly or a foul ball is caught.
   b. The catcher tags.
   c. He strikes out.
6. When a batter is put out, the players rotate positions:
   a. The batter becomes the fielder.
   b. The fielder becomes the pitcher.
   c. The pitcher becomes the catcher.
   d. The catcher becomes the batter.

192—Zoo

Playing Area: Classroom
Players: Entire class
Equipment: None

1. Six students stand in front of the class and choose the name of an animal to imitate.
2. The teacher puts the children in a line, saying the name of the animal.
3. While staying in their assigned line, the children imitate their animals for about 20 seconds.
4. The rest of the children jump around, wave their arms, and sit down in their desks with their hands covering their eyes.
5. The teacher changes the order of the six zoo animals, and the children in their seats can look while the animals imitate once again.
6. Now the seated children attempt to put the zoo animals in their original line and guess the name of each animal.
7. If a child correctly names and places the zoo animals, he becomes a zoo animal.

Rhythmical Activities

Rhythm is a "pattern of movement or sound" and can be found often in nature. Feel your heart beating; watch the trees bending; hear the wind blowing; consider the changing seasons. Children's natural instinct for rhythm should be encouraged early. In dance, rhythm is of regular occurrence and ordered sequence. Development of rhythm in dance is dependent on body structure, motor proficiency, kinesthetic sense, concentration, ability to synchronize movement, and accompaniment.

Rhythmic Patterns

Begin with patterns of two speeds. Combine moderate and fast intervals or moderate and slow intervals; then make patterns of three speeds.

Movement Patterns for Names

Use of nursery rhymes, jingles, and radio and television commercials stimulates creation of a sequence of movement patterns and is excellent for beginning creative work. Perform rounds in movement. Group decides on movement pattern for a familiar round; group divides into parts and dances as a round.

Accent

Leader arranges beats of established interval, accenting the first of each series. Repeat each series to let children get the "feel" of it; have them clap the rhythm before moving. Encourage use of locomotor and body movements.

Directions:
1. Respond to accented beats only.
2. Respond to a series of beats with a strong movement on the accents, or a change of level or direction on the accents.
3. Respond to unaccented beats only. Syncopated movement results.
4. Work with partner: Number One responds to the accent; Number Two responds to the succeeding beats.

Group Patterns

Two groups work in opposition, with one group showing accented movements and the other responding to the succeeding beats.

Band Conductors

The class works out movements for leading the band, using a downbeat of the hands for each accented beat. Try walking and conducting. This requires advanced coordination of hands and feet. Use various meters.

Dance in the elementary level comprises two main divisions: creative dance and the social forms of dance. Creative dance is feeling expressed in movement. The latter includes folk, square, round, and social dances. A common approach is possible in teaching all forms of dancing. This approach includes (1) the creative development of movement and rhythm skills basic to all dance forms, (2) an encouraging, permissive atmosphere, which contributes to all creative endeavor, and (3) carefully planned dance activities that grow out of the daily experiences and immediate needs and interests of the children.

Creative Dance

Creative dance experiences grow out of immediate interests and daily experiences of children. A study of Indian life, a favorite story, seasonal music, or a unit in social studies may provide a theme for movement and rhythm problems.

Directions:
1. Decide on an idea.
2. Plan the dance.
3. Decide on floor pattern or design of the dance.
4. Decide on accompaniment.
5. Perform and evaluate the dance.

Phrases

A phrase consists of four or eight measures in simple music. Establish by questioning the children: What is a sentence? A sentence expresses a thought in words. How do you express a thought in movement? Listen to familiar music; show the beginning and ending of the phrase by extending and lowering your hands, now your whole body.

Dance Positions

Closed. This is the social dance position. The boy faces the girl, holding her right hand in his left out to the side at shoulder height with elbows bent. His right hand is on the girl's back just below her left shoulder blade. Her left arm rests on his right arm with her hand on his shoulder.

Open. From closed position, boy turns to his left and girl to her right. Both are facing same direction and are side by side.

Varsouvienne. Stand side by side facing same direction. Boy holds girl's left hand in his left in front. She brings her right hand over her right shoulder and the boy grasps this hand with his right behind her back.

Peasant. This is also called the waist-shoulder position. Partners face each other, and boy puts his hands on girl's waist. Girl puts her hands on his shoulders.

Square Dancing

This activity is fun and a challenge to children who are 11 or 12 years of age. Basic skills should be simple and a challenge but not a chore to the children. The basic step is the shuffle. It consists of a quick, light slide in time to the music. The parts of square dancing are:

(1) Introduction
(2) The main figure (name of dance)
(3) Breaks (trimmings, fill-ins, chorus)
(4) Ending

Record companies used in this book:
Educational Record Center, 3120 Maple Dr., STE 124, Atlanta, GA 30305
Hoctor Educational Records, Inc., Waldwick, NJ 07463
Kimbo Educational Records, P.O. Box 477, Long Branch, NJ 07740
Worldtone Music, Inc., 230 7th Ave., New York, NY 10011

Mimetics

The child takes on the identity of an object or a person. While using rhythm, he interprets this identity. The rhythms are divided into identification and dramatic groups. For example, the child can identify himself with:

a. Animals—elephants, ducks, seals, chickens, cats, rabbits, etc.
b. People—soldiers, Indians, clowns, firemen, sailors, workers, etc.
c. Play Objects—seesaws, swings, rowboats, balls, toys, etc.
d. Make-Believe World—fairies, dwarfs, witches, giants, dragons, pixies, etc.
e. Machines—trains, planes, automobiles, elevators, tractors, etc.

The child can act out the following ideas, stories, and events:

a. Building a house, garage, or other project.
b. Making a snowman, throwing snowballs, going skiing.
c. Flying a kite, going hunting or fishing, going camping.
d. Acting out stories which include Indians, cowboys, firemen, engineers.
e. Interpreting familiar stories like "Sleeping Beauty," "The Three Bears," "Little Red Riding Hood," and others.
f. Building from household chores like chopping wood, picking fruit, mowing the lawn, cleaning the yard.
g. Celebrating holidays like Halloween, Fourth of July, Thanksgiving, Christmas.

197—Ace of Diamonds
(Folkcraft 1176)

1. Form a double circle; boys inside.
2. Clap hands, hook partner's right arm, walk clockwise 6 steps.
3. Clap hands, hook partner's left arm, walk counterclockwise.
4. Fold arms and take 4 step-hops to center; 4 step-hops back.
5. Join hands and polka counterclockwise around the circle.

198—Ach Ja
(Worldtone)

1. Form a double circle, boys inside; all face counterclockwise, join hands.
2. 8 steps, drop hands and bow.
3. Each boy bows to girl on left.
4. Partners take 4 slides in line of direction; 4 slides back and bow.
5. Boy bows to girl on left; she is his new partner.

VERSE:
"When my father and mother
take the children to the fair,
Ach Ja! Ach Ja!
Oh, they have but little money,
But it's little that they care,
Ach Ja! Ach Ja!
Tra la la, Tra la la, Tra la la
La la la la
Tra la la, Tra la la, Tra la la
La la la la
Ach Ja! Ach Ja!"

199—A Hunting We Will Go
(Folkcraft F1191 or Worldtone)

1. Girls in one line, boys in another.
2. First couple slides between the lines to the end and back again.
3. Couples skip in a circle until first couple is at end of line.
4. First couple forms an arch and others skip under; new head couple begins dance again.

VERSE:
"Oh, a-hunting we will go,
A-hunting we will go,
We'll catch a fox and put him in a box
And then we'll let him go!"

CHORUS:
"Tra, la, la, la, la, la, la, etc."

200—Baa, Baa Black Sheep
(Worldtone)
1. Form a circle, face center.
2. Stamp three times, shake forefinger three times.
3. Twice nod head; put up three fingers.
4. Bow to person on right and then to left.
5. Walk in a small circle with one finger up, and face center again.

VERSE:
"Baa, Baa, Black Sheep
Have you any wool?
Yes sir, yes sir, three bags full.
One for my master and one for my dame.
And one for the little boy
who lives down the lane."

201—Balance Step
1. Left step to side.
2. Right close.
3. Left step in place.
4. Reverse steps 1, 2, & 3.

202—Ball Skill in Rhythm
1. Bounce and catch.
2. Throwing or volleying against a wall.
3. Dribbling (continuous bouncing).
4. Passing a ball from person to person in rhythm.

203—Bleking
(Folkcraft 1188 or Worldtone)
1. Single circle, hands joined.
2. Hop on left foot; right leg straight and forward; right hand forward.
3. Reverse action; left, right, left.
4. Extend joined hands shoulder high.
5. 16 step-hops clockwise; move arms up and down as a windmill.

204—Broom Dance
(Worldtone)
1. Double circle, boys on inside; extra boy with broom in center.
2. Partners march counterclockwise, boys handing broom around.
3. Boy with broom at end of verse sweeps in center during chorus.
4. End of chorus, boys move forward to next girl; verse begins new game.

VERSE:
"1, 2, 3, 4, 5, 6, 7
Where's my partner, 9, 10, 11?
In Berlin, in Stettin,
There's the place to find him in."

CHORUS:
"Tra la, la, etc."

205—Brown-Eyed Mary Mixer
(Folkcraft 1186)
Formation: Couples face counterclockwise, boys on inside, right hands and left hands joined in crossed position.
1. Two-step left and two-step right, walk forward four steps.
2. Repeat step one.
3. Boy takes girl's right hand in his right and walks around partner to face girl behind him.
4. Turns girl behind him with the left.
5. Turns own partner with right going all the way around.
6. Boy moves one step up to girl who is his new partner.

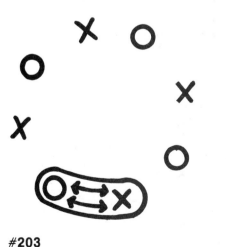

#203

#205

206—Carrousel
(Worldtone or Folkcraft 1183)
1. Double circle, all facing inward. Inner circle joins hands. Outer circle has hands on hips.
2. Begin with slow draw step to the left.
3. Stamp on **bold** words of verse.
4. During chorus, a faster slide develops. Repeat chorus sliding in other direction.

VERSE:
"Little children, sweet and gay,
Carrousel is running,
It will run to evening,
Little ones a nickel, big ones a dime
Hurry **up**, get a **mate**,
Or you'll **surely** be too **late**."

CHORUS:
"Ha, ha, ha, happy are we,
Anderson and Peterson and Henderson and me,
Ha, ha, ha happy are we,
Anderson and Peterson and Henderson and me."

207—Children's Polka
(Worldtone or Folkcraft 1187)
1. One circle, partners facing with hands joined.
2. Two draw steps to center and stamp 3 times.
3. Repeat, moving away from center.
4. Repeat 2 and 3.
5. Clap thighs once, partner's hands three times — and repeat.
6. Put right foot forward, right elbow in left hand and shake forefinger 3 times.
7. Repeat 6 reversed.
8. Turn around in 4 running steps and stamp 3 times.

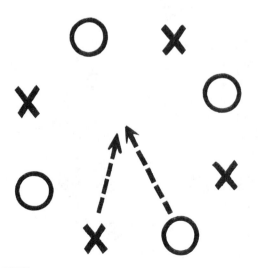

#207

208—Chimes of Dunkirk
(Worldtone or Folkcraft 1188)
1. Single circle, partners facing.
2. Stamp lightly, left, right, left.
3. Clap hands overhead.
4. With partner, join hands and turn once clockwise.
5. Circle joins hands and slides to left 16 times.

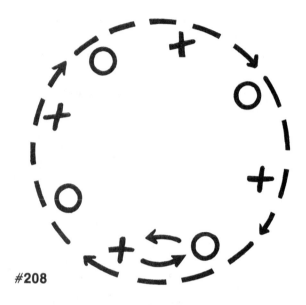

#208

209—Circle Stoop
1. March to music in a single circle, counter-clockwise.
2. When music stops all touch both hands to floor.
3. Last one down is eliminated.

210—Circle Virginia Reel
(Worldtone or Folkcraft 1249)
1. Double circle with partners facing, boys inside.
2. Listen to calls.
3. Change partners with "On to the next" — boys go to left.

CALLS:
"Forward and back,
Right hand swing,
Left hand swing,
Both hands swing,
Dos-a-dos your partner,
Right elbow swing,
Left elbow swing,
Swing your partner,
On to the next."

211—Come Let Us Be Joyful
(Folkcraft 1195 or Worldtone)
1. Sets of three in a circle with boy in center and girls on outside.
2. Lines of three, three steps forward and bow. Three steps back and close with feet together.
3. Repeat 1 and 2.
4. Middle boy in each set hooks (elbows) arms with partner on right and swings, four skipping steps.
5. Repeat 4 with partner on left.
6. Repeat 2. Don't bow. Lines move forward and pass through the opposite line, passing by right shoulders to form a new line.

213—Csebogar
(Worldtone or Folkcraft 1196)
1. Single circle, hands joined.
2. Left, 7 slides, right, 7 slides.
3. 4 skips to center and 4 skips back.
4. Hook partner's arm and swing twice around.
5. Partners face, hands joined.
6. 4 draw steps to center and 4 back.
7. 2 draw steps to center and 2 back.
8. Hook elbows, swing, shout, and end facing in.

212—Crested Hen
(Worldtone)
1. Sets of three, two boys and a girl.
2. Each set begins with a stamp to the left and then step-hops.
3. Jump and reverse.
4. Girl on right step-hops under arch formed by other two. Boy unravels line by turning his left arm.
5. Repeat 4 with girl on left.

214—Dance of Greeting
(Folkcraft 1188 or Worldtone)
1. Single circle, face center.
2. Clap twice and bow to partner.
3. Clap twice and bow to neighbor.
4. Stamp left and right, turn around in 4 running steps.
5. Repeat 2, 3, and 4.
6. Join hands and run forward 16 steps and back 16 steps.

215—Dance Steps
1. Step-Hop—step right and hop on same leg; repeat on left leg.
2. Polka—left step, right close, left step, left hop and reverse.
3. Schottische—(1) left step, right step, left step, left hop and reverse (2) 4 step-hops and repeat (1).
4. Two Step—left step, right close, left step and reverse.
5. Waltz—left step, right step, left close and reverse.
6. Waltz Balance—left step forward, close right and hold; back step right, left close and hold.

216—Did You Ever See a Lassie?
(Worldtone or Folkcraft 1183)
1. Join hands in circle and walk to beat of music.
2. Child in center demonstrates a movement.
3. Circle stops and follows movement of center child.
4. With new verse, child in center selects a new one.

VERSE:

"Did you ever see a lassie,
a lassie, a lassie?
Did you ever see a lassie
do this way and that?
Do this way and that way, and
this way and that way.
Did you ever see a lassie do
this way and that."

218—Farmer in the Dell
(Folkcraft 1182 or Worldtone)
1. Single circle, hands joined.
2. One child is farmer.
3. Circle walks to left continuously.
4. Each verse another child is picked to go to the center by preceding child (as wife, child, nurse, etc.).
5. "Cheese" becomes the new farmer at the end of the song and begins over again.

VERSES:

"The farmer in the dell,
The farmer in the dell.
Heigh-O! The dairy-O!
The farmer in the dell."
a. "The farmer takes a wife."
b. "The wife takes a child."
c. "The child takes a nurse."
d. "The nurse takes a dog."
e. "The dog takes a cat."
f. "The cat takes a rat."
g. "The rat takes the cheese."
h. "The cheese stands alone."

220—Freeze
1. Children are scattered.
2. During music they move about in any way they wish.
3. They must stop when music stops; if not they pay a penalty.

217—Exercise to Rhythms
1. Groups practice same exercise.
2. Groups practice different exercises and rotate on signal.
3. Separate groups are picked and children assigned according to capabilities.
4. Groups practice varied skills; children go to group they want.

219—Follow Me
1. Circle facing child in center.
2. Center child demonstrates — circle children imitate.
3. New leader is picked.
4. Demonstrations follow music.

221—Fundamental Rhythms
Locomotor Movements:
Even Rhythms — walk, run, leap, hop, jump
Uneven Rhythms — skip, slide, gallop
Nonlocomotor Movements:
Simple — turn, bend, swing, twist, sway, fall
Mimetic — strike, lift, push, pull, throw
Elements in Music Listening:
Tempo, intensity, accent, meter, beat

222—Glow Worm Mixer
(Worldtone or Folkcraft 1158)

1. Double circle, partners join inside hands.
2. Forward 4 steps.
3. Face partner and back 4 steps.
4. Boys walk 4 steps to girl in couple ahead.
5. Join elbows and swing.
6. Join hands and repeat, boys change partners around the circle.

223—Go Round and Round the Village

1. Single circle, hands joined.
2. Other players scattered outside the circle.
3. Circle players to right and outside players to left, all skipping.
4. Circle players lift arms for windows and others go in and out, ending inside of circle.
5. Extra players stand in front of a partner.
6. Partners skip around inside of circle and outside circle skips in opposite direction.

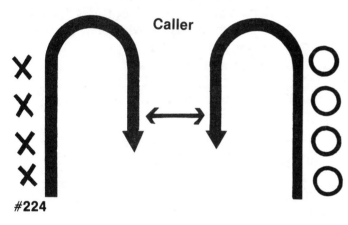

#224

225—Greensleeves
(Folkcraft 6175)

1. Couples form a circle, all facing counterclockwise. Boys are on the inside and inside hands are joined. Two couples form a set, #1 and #2.
2. During the first eight measures of the record the couples walk forward for 16 steps.
3. Couple #1 turns so that they are facing the couple behind them during measures nine to twelve. They all join right hands and circle clockwise for 8 steps.
4. During the playing of measures thirteen to sixteen the couples reverse and join left hands and circle counterclockwise bringing couple #1 back to its original place.
5. While measures seventeen to twenty-four are being played, couple #2 forms an arch with their hands and couple #1 backs under with 4 steps while couple #2 goes forward 4 steps. Now couple #1 forms an arch and couple #2 backs under it with 4 steps.

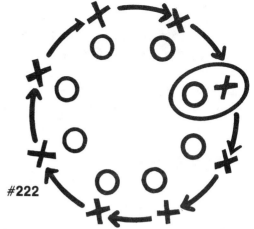

#222

VERSE:
"Go round and round the village (3 times)
As we have done before."
 a. "Go in and out the windows, etc."
 b. "Now stand and face your partner, etc."
 c. "Now follow me to London, etc."

224—Grand March

1. Girls on left face caller, boys on right end.
2. Lines march to caller and proceed down center in couples.
3. Odd couples left, even couples right.
4. Down center again 4 across facing caller.
5. Odd couples left and even couples right.
6. Meet at foot. Odd couples form arch and even couples go under.
7. All couples go through and meet at head again.
8. Odd couples form arch and repeat 6.
9. Meet at foot and proceed 4 across down center to head.
10. 4's go left and right alternating and meet at foot.
11. 8 across and down center.
12. All join hands in each line and form one large line marching around.

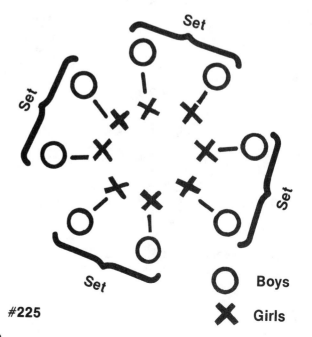

#225

◯ Boys

✕ Girls

53

226—Gustaf's Skoal
(Worldtone or Folkcraft F1175)

1. Form a square composed of four couples; partners have inside hands joined, with the boy on the left of his partner. Two of the couples are said to be the "head couples" while the other two couples facing one another are the "side couples."

2. During measures:

1-4 "Head couples" walk forward for three steps, bow and return to place with three steps; during this "side couples" hold their places.

5-8 "Side couples" do the same, while "head couples" hold places.

1-4 Repeat movements of measures 1-4 above.

5-8 Repeat movements of measures 5-8 above.

9-12 "Side couples" raise hands to form an arch. "Head couples" skip to center with four skips. Each, after dropping his own partner's hands, joins hands with the dancer facing him and skips with new partner under the nearest arch.

13-14 After going under the arch, drop hands with opposite and head back to home spot to original partner.

15-16 All partners hook right elbows and skip around the circle with four skipping steps.

9-16 Repeat movements of measures 9-16 of the above with "head couples" forming the arches.

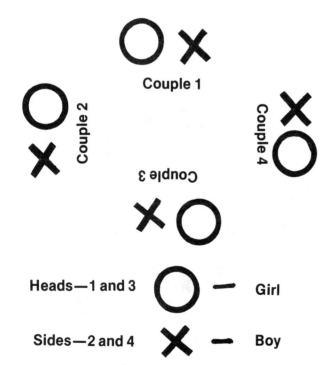

Couple 1

Couple 2

Couple 3

Couple 4

Heads—1 and 3   Girl

Sides—2 and 4   Boy

#226

227—Hansel and Gretel
(Worldtone or Folkcraft 1193)

1. Form a double circle, partners facing with boys on the inside.

2. During measures:

1-2 Boys bow and girls curtsy.

3-4 Give partner both hands in crossed arm position, right hand to right hand and left to left.

5-6 Jump and extend forward the right heel; then do the same with the left heel.

7-8 Each child turns around in a circle with seven fast light steps.

9-16 Partners join hands and with sixteen skips go around the circle with inside hands joined.

17 Partners face and place hands on hips.

18 Stamp three times right, left, right.

19 Stand still facing partner, hands on hips.

20 Clap hands three times.

21-24 Repeat movements of measures 5-8 above. Repeat entire dance with the exception of measures 18, 19, 20.

18 Nod head three times.

19 Stand still with hands on hips.

20 Snap fingers hard three times.

VERSE:
"Partner come and dance with me,
Both your hands now give to me,
Right foot first, left foot then,
Round and round and back again.
Right foot first, left foot then,
Round and round and back again."
CHORUS:
"Tra la la la la la la
(Repeat)
Let your feet go stamp, stamp, stamp,
Let your hands go clap, clap, clap,
Right foot first, left foot then,
Round and round and back again.
Let your head go nip, nip, nip,
Let your fingers go snip, snip, snip,
Right foot first, left foot then,
Round and round and back again."

228—Heel and Toe Polka
(Worldtone or Folkcraft 1484)

These directions are for boys. Girls use opposite foot.

1. Form a double circle, all facing counterclockwise. Boys occupy the inside and all partners hold hands.
2. In measures:

   1-2 With weight on the inside foot, bring the outside heel forward on the floor. On "toe," bring the toe alongside the instep. During this time the weight is still on the inside foot. Step left, right, left.

   3-4 With weight on the outside foot, repeat the measures 1-2 beginning with the inside heel and toe. Step right, left, right.

   5-6 Repeat measures 1-2 above.

   7-8 Repeat measures 3-4 above.

   9-16 With inside hands joined and partners side by side, do 8 two-steps in line of direction.

229—Hickory Dickory Dock
(Worldtone or Folkcraft V22760)

1. Children are in a double circle formation, with partners facing.
2. In line:

   1 Bring arms overhead and bend the body from side to side like a pendulum, finishing with two stamps of the feet on "tick, tock."

   2 Repeat movements of line one.

   3 Clap hands on one. Join hands with partners and run to the right in a circle.

   4 Repeat the pendulum action as in line 1 with the two stamps of the feet.

VERSE:

"Hickory, Dickory, Dock, tick tock,
The mouse ran up the clock, tick tock.
The clock struck one; the mouse ran down.
Hickory, Dickory, Dock, tick tock."

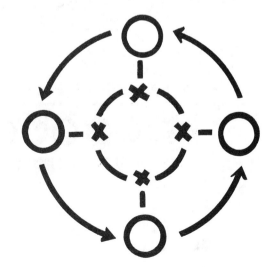

 Boys

#230

230—Horse and Buggy Schottischie
(Folkcraft 1166)

1. Couples are in sets of four in a double circle, all facing counterclockwise. Couples join inside hands and give outside hands to the other couple.
2. During the first part all run forward with a step, step, step, hop; step, step, step, hop.
3. During the four step-hops, one of two movements can be done:

   a. The first couple could drop inside hands and step-hops around the outside of the back couple, who in turn goes forward during the step-hops. The first couple now joins hands behind the other couple and the positions are reversed.

   b. The first couple with hands joined moves backward under the upraised hands of the back couple, who untwists by turning away from one another.

   c. Alternate 1 and 2.

55

231—How D'Ye Do, My Partner?
(Worldtone or Folkcraft 1190)

1. Double circle formation, with boys on the inside and partners facing each other.
2. In measures:
    - 1-2 Boys bow to partners.
    - 3-4 Girls curtsy to partners.
    - 5-6 Boys and girls join hands in crossed-arm position, right hand to right hand and left to left. Both turn to counterclockwise position.
    - 7-8 Get ready to skip.
    - 1-8 Partners skip counterclockwise in the circle slowing down on measure 7. On the last measure the children in the outside circle skip forward to meet a new partner.

VERSE:

"How d'ye do, my partner?
How d'ye do, today?
Will you dance in the circle?
I will show you the way.
Tra la la la la la
Tra la la la la
Tra la la la la la
And I thank you, good day."

233—Jolly Is the Miller
(Worldtone or Folkcraft 1192)

1. Form a double circle with partners' inside hands joined, facing counterclockwise. Boys are on the inside with a child in the center of the circle acting as the Miller.
2. Now the double circle skips forward during the first 3 lines of the song.
3. During the second line when "wheel goes around" the dancers should make their outside arms go in a circle to form a wheel.
4. On the fourth line the boys leave their partners and reverse direction; the girls continue skipping forward.
5. The "Miller" then has a chance to get a partner. The child left without a partner then becomes the "Miller."

VERSE:

"Jolly is the Miller, who lives by the mill;
The wheel goes round with a right good will,
One hand on the hopper and the other on the sack;
The right steps forward and the left steps back."

232—I See You
(Worldtone or Folkcraft 1197)

1. Form two double lines facing each other. Each player in back of partner has his hands on his partner's waist.
2. In measures:
    - 1 Active players look over the partner's left shoulder.
    - 2 Look over partner's right shoulder.
    - 3-4 On the "tra la la's" the speed of the looking over the partner's shoulder is doubled so the child looks over left and right in each measure.
    - 5-8 Repeat measures 1-4 above.
    - 9-12 All children clap at the first note of the measure and the active players, passing to the left of their partners, meet in the center with a two-handed swing, skipping around once in a circle, clockwise.
    - 13-16 All children clap on the first note and the active player now faces his own partner and with a two-handed swing makes a clockwise turn with his partner. Partners now have changed places, and a new set of active players are ready for a new dance.

VERSE:

"I see you, I see you,
Tra la la la la la la la.
I see you, I see you,
Tra la la la la la.
You see me and I see you,
And you take me and I take you;
You see me and I see you,
And you take me and I take you."

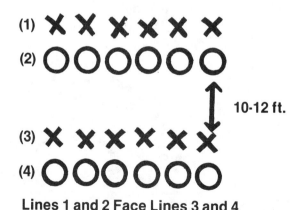

(1) ✗ ✗ ✗ ✗ ✗ ✗
(2) ◯◯◯◯◯◯

↕ 10-12 ft.

(3) ✗ ✗ ✗ ✗ ✗ ✗
(4) ◯◯◯◯◯◯

Lines 1 and 2 Face Lines 3 and 4

◯ Girls
✗ Boys

#232

234—Jump, Jim Joe
(Folkcraft 1180 or Worldtone)

1. Form a double circle with partners facing. Join both hands with boys on the inside.
2. During measures:
   1 Two slow and three fast jumps in place.
   2 Partners run around each other in clockwise position in a circle and then return to original position.
   3 Now the children place hands on hips and move to their left with two draw steps (step left, close right, step left, close right) then do three stamps. Each child now has a new partner.
   4 Join hands with your new partner and run around each other back to place.
   5 Finish with three light jumps on the words, "Jump, Jim Joe."

VERSE:
"Jump, jump, and jump, Jim Joe,
Take a little twirl and away we go,
Slide, slide, and stamp just so — and
Take another partner and jump, Jim Joe."

236—La Raspa
(Worldtone or Folkcraft 1457)

1. No definite formation. It's a couple's dance with couples scattered around the room.
2. During measures:
   1-4 Partners face in opposite ways standing left shoulder to left shoulder. Boy joins his hands behind his back while girl holds her skirt. Do one Bleking step, beginning with right foot.
   5-8 Partners now face other way with right shoulder to right shoulder. Do one Bleking step, beginning with left foot.
   9-16 Repeat measures 1-8.
   17-20 Join right elbows, turning with 8 running steps. On the eighth step clap your hands.
   21-24 Join left elbows, and turn your partner again with 8 steps. Clap hands on eighth step.
   25-32 Repeat measures 17-24 as stated above.

235—Klappdans
(Worldtone: World of Fun #7)

1. Double circle, all facing counterclockwise. Boys on the inside. Inside hands are joined with other hand on the hip.
2. During measures:
   1-8 Starting on outside foot, partners polka around the circle.
   9-16 Do a heel and toe polka, leaning back "heel" and forward on "toe".
   17-20 Partners face and bow to each other. Then clap three times. Repeat again.
   21-22 Clap partner's right hand, own hands, partner's left hand, and again your own hands.
   23 Make a turn in your place in the left, clapping right hand against right hand while turning.
   24 Stamp feet three times.
   25-32 Repeat measures 17-24.

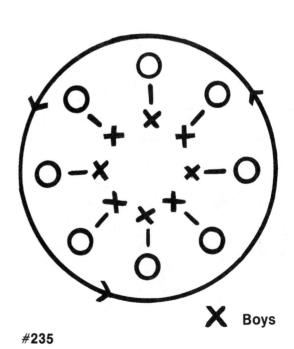

X Boys

#235

57

237—Little Brown Jug
(Worldtone or Folkcraft 1167)

These directions are for boys; girls use opposite foot.

1. Form a double circle with partners facing and boys occupying the inside. Partners join hands.
2. During measures:

1-4 Boys touch left toe to the side and bring the foot back beside the right foot. Run out again. Repeat. Now do three slides to the left and bring feet together.

5-8 Do the same as in measures 1-4 but use the opposite foot so that you go in the opposite direction. This should bring the partners back to their original position.

9-12 All clap hands to thighs three times. Clap partner's left hand three times. Clap partner's right hand three times. Partners clap both hands three times.

13-14 Partners join right elbows and skip around until boy faces the next girl, the one who was on the boy's right in the original position.

15-16 The boy now joins elbows with the new girl and skips completely around her with a left elbow swing, goes back to the middle of circle, and repeats the dance again.

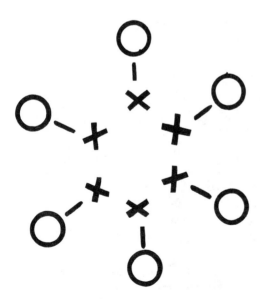

 Boys

#237

238—London Bridge
(Worldtone or Folkcraft 6151)

1. Form a single circle facing inward, with two children chosen to form a bridge.
2. The two children who form the bridge have agreed upon two objects, each child taking one. The children pass under the bridge in a single line. When they sing the words "My fair lady," the two keepers of the bridge let their arms fall and catch a player. The one caught must then choose which object he prefers, and then stand behind the player whose object he chose.
3. When all the children have been caught, there is a tug-of-war.

VERSES:

1. "London Bridge is falling down, Falling down, falling down, London Bridge is falling down, My fair lady."
2. "Build it up with iron bars."
3. "Iron bars will rust away."
4. "Build it up with gold and silver."
5. "Gold and silver I have not."
6. "Build it up with pins and needles."
7. "Pins and needles rust and bend."
8. "Build it up with penny loaves."
9. "Penny loaves will tumble down."
10. "Here's a prisoner I have got."
11. "What's the prisoner done to you?"
12. "Stole my watch and bracelet, too."
13. "What'll you take to set him free?"
14. "100 pounds will set him free."
15. "100 pounds we don't have."
16. "Then off to prison he the must go."

#239

239—Long Rope Jumping

The rope should be 16 to 18 feet long and approximately ½ inch in diameter.

1. Divide children into groups of 5, so that two of the group are turners and the other three are jumpers.
2. Introductory skills:
   a. Hold the rope 6 inches from the floor and let the children jump over it.
   b. Swing the rope back and forth like a pendulum, letting the children jump over the swinging rope.
   c. Have the three jumpers stand in the center between the two turners. Turn the rope in a circle over the jumpers' heads. As the rope completes the circle, the jumpers jump the rope.
   d. Turners turn the rope while the jumper runs in, jumps, and runs out.
   e. Turners hold the rope in their hands and gradually raise the height of the rope. Jumpers jump the rope and continue until the height is beyond their capacity.
   f. The turners make waves in the rope by moving their hands up and down. The jumpers attempt to jump over the waves.

241—March Attack

Playing Area: Playground, gym with two parallel lines drawn 60 feet apart
Players: Two teams, 15 to 40 on each
Equipment: None

1. One team is on one of the parallel lines with backs to the area between the lines. These are the chasers.
2. The other team is on the other line facing the area. This is the marching team.
3. The marching team goes forward on signal toward the chasers. When they get close, a signal (a whistle) is given and the marchers turn and

240—Looby Loo
(Folkcraft 1184)

1. Form a single circle facing inward with hands joined.
2. During the chorus the children skip around the circle. With each verse the children stand still facing the center and follow the directions of the words.
3. On the words "And turn myself about" they make a complete turn in place.

CHORUS:

"Here we dance looby loo,
Here we dance looby light
Here we dance looby loo
All on a Saturday night."

(Repeat before each verse.)

VERSE 1:

"I put my right hand in
I take my right hand out
I give my right hand a shake, shake, shake,
And turn myself about."

VERSES:

2. "I put my left hand in, etc."
3. "I put my right foot in, etc."
4. "I put my left foot in, etc."
5. "I put my head way in, etc."
6. "I put my whole self in, etc."

run back to their line, chased by the other team. If any of the marchers are caught by the chasers before they reach their line, they become members of the other team.

4. The game is repeated again with the marchers becoming the chasers, and the chasers becoming the marchers.

242—Muffin Man
(Folkcraft F1188)

1. Form a single circle, facing the center, with hands joined. One child, representing the Muffin Man, is in the center.
2. During verses:
    1 The children in the circle stand still and sing while the Muffin Man skips around the circle. As the words "who lives in Drury Lane" are sung, the center child chooses a partner.
    2 During this verse the action is the same as verse 1 except now there are two people in the center of the circle skipping around and each of them chooses a partner.
    3 During this verse the action is the same as the preceding verses except now there are four people in the center of the circle and each of these chooses a partner.
    4 The verses continue until all the children in the circle have been chosen. When all the children have been chosen, the last verse of the song is sung with the children skipping around the room.

VERSES:
1. "Oh, do you know the muffin man,
    the muffin man, the muffin man?
    Oh, do you know the muffin man,
    Who lives in Drury Lane?"
2. "Oh, yes, we know the muffin man, etc."
3. "Four of us know the muffin man, etc."
4. "Eight of us know the muffin man, etc."
5. "Sixteen of us know the muffin man, etc."
6. "All of us know the muffin man, etc."

VERSES:
1. "This is the way we wash our clothes,
    Wash our clothes, wash our clothes,
    This is the way we wash our clothes
    So early Monday morning."
2. "This is the way we iron our clothes,
    (Tuesday morning)"
3. "This is the way we mend our clothes,
    (Wednesday morning)"
4. "This is the way we sweep our floor,
    (Thursday morning)"
5. "This is the way we scrub our floor,
    (Friday morning)"
6. "This is the way we make a cake,
    (Saturday morning)"
7. "This is the way we go to church,
    (Sunday morning)"

243—Mulberry Bush
(Worldtone or Folkcraft 1183)

1. Form a single circle, facing inward, with hands joined.
2. During the singing of the chorus the children skip to the right. On the words "so early in the morning," each child drops hands and makes a complete circle.
3. During the verses the children imitate the words.

CHORUS:
    "Here we go around the mulberry bush,
    The mulberry bush, the mulberry bush,
    Here we go around the mulberry bush,
    So early in the morning."

60

244—Patty Cake Polka
(Folkcraft or Worldtone)

These directions are for boys; girls use opposite foot.

1. Form a double circle made up of couples with the boys having their backs to the center of the circle and both hands joined to their partners, who are facing them.
2. Part 1: Heel, toe, heel, toe, slide, slide, slide (step with the left foot out on the heel, bring the left foot back on the toe and slide three steps to the left). This is the boys' part. Girls use opposite foot.
3. Part 2: Boys use right foot this time and girls use left. Heel, toe, heel, toe, slide, slide, slide.
4. Part 3: Still facing partners, clap each other's right hand, then left hand, then both hands, your own knees and join right hands and turn around.
5. Commands for caller: Heel and toe, heel and toe, slide, slide, slide. Heel and toe, heel and toe, slide, slide, slide. With the right clap, clap, left clap, clap, both clap, clap, knees clap, clap. Swing your partner once around (2 measures).
6. To change partners, after the swing have the boys move forward, one partner counterclockwise and girls wait for new partner.

245—Norwegian Mountain March
(Worldtone or Folkcraft 1177)

1. Form sets made up of one boy and two girls. The boy stands in front and the two girls stand behind him in triangle formation. The girls hold inside hands and the boy reaches back to take the girls' outside hands.

   This dance portrays a guide leading two mountain climbers up a mountain. Throughout the entire dance the dancers keep their hands joined.
2. In measures:
   1-8 The children run forward 24 steps.
   9-16 Repeat the action from measures 1-8.
   17-18 The boy goes backward under the girls' raised arms, for 6 steps.
   19-20 The girl on the boy's left takes 6 steps to cross in front of the boy and to go under his raised right arm.
   21-22 The girl on the boy's right takes six steps and turns under the boy's right arm.
   23-24 Now the boy goes under his own arm and the boy and girls should be in their original position.
   25-32 A repeat of measures 17 to 24 is made except that the girls and boy turn under the boy's left arm.

246—Oats, Peas, Beans and Barley Grow
(Worldtone or Folkcraft 1182)

1. Form a single circle with hands joined. Have one child in the center representing a "farmer."
2. During verses:
   1 All children walk clockwise around the farmer.
   2 They stop and imitate the words of the verses.
   3 Children move again clockwise while the "farmer" takes a partner.
   4 The circle skips clockwise and the "farmer" and his partner skip counterclockwise.

VERSES:

1. "Oats, peas, beans, and barley grow,
   Oats, peas, beans, and barley grow
   You and I, or anyone know, how
   Oats, peas, beans, and barley grow?
2. First, the farmer sows the seed,
   Then he stands and takes his ease,
   He stamps his foot and claps his hands
   And turns around to view his lands.
3. Waiting for a partner,
   Waiting for a partner,
   Open the ring and choose one in
   While we all gaily dance and sing.
4. Now you're married, you must obey
   You must be kind in all you say
   You must be kind, you must be good,
   And keep your wife in kindling wood."

248—Oh Johnny, Oh
(Folkcraft 1037 or Worldtone)

1. Form a set made up of 4 couples.
2. Action:
   a. Circle of eight move to the left.
   b. Swing your partner.
   c. Swing the corner lady (on man's left).
   d. Swing your partner again.
   e. Turn the corner lady with the left hand.
   f. Walk around your partner passing right shoulders and back to place.
   g. Promenade with your new partner (lady on your left).
3. The dance is usually done four times in all, so that original partners are together again at the end.

   Call (all sing):
   a. All join hands and you circle the ring.
   b. Stop where you are and you give her a swing.
   c. Now you swing that girl behind you.
   d. Now swing your own if you have time.
   e. Allemande left on your corners all.
   f. All dos-a-dos your own.
   g. And all promenade with the sweet corner maid singing, "Oh Johnny, Oh Johnny, Oh!"

249—Oh Susanna
(Folkcraft 1186 or Worldtone)

1. Couples form a single circle facing inward with the girl on the boy's right, all hands joined.
2. During measures:
   1-4 All take 8 sliding steps to the right.
   5-8 All take 8 sliding steps to the left.
   9-12 Four skips to the center and four back.
   13-16 Partners face each other and join right hands, walk past each other so that right shoulders pass and give your left hand to the next child. (This is called grand right and left.) The next child is your new partner.
   17-24 Promenade the circle.

250—Partner Stoop

1. Partners form a double circle facing counter-clockwise, with the boys on the inside.
2. When music begins all march in the same direction.
3. After a while a signal (a whistle), is given and the inside circle of boys turns around and marches clockwise.
4. When the music stops, the girls stand still and the boys move on to join their partners.
5. As soon as the partners meet they join inside hands and stoop without losing their balance.
6. The last couple to stoop goes to the middle of the circle and waits out the next round.

251—Paw Paw Patch
(Worldtone or Folkcraft 1181)
1. Children are in groups of four to eight couples. Boys are in one line and girls in another on the boys' right, all facing forward.
2. During verse:
    1 Head girl turns to her right and skips around the entire group of children while the other children remain in their places and sing.
    2 The first girl turns to her right again and this time she is followed by the entire line of boys who beckon to one another.
    3 Partners now join inside hands and skip in a circle to the right following the lead couple. When the lead couple is at the end of the line, they make an arch under which the other couples skip back to their original places, with a new lead couple.
3. Repeat the dance until each couple has had the opportunity to be the lead couple.
    VERSES:
    1. "Where, Oh where is sweet little Nellie,
    Where, Oh where is sweet little Nellie,
    Where, Oh where is sweet little Nellie,
    Way down yonder in the paw paw patch.
    2. Come on, boys, let's go find her, etc.
    3. Pickin' up paw paw's, puttin' in your basket, etc.''

252—Polka Steps
Any polka record
1. Step left, close right, step forward left, hop left.
2. Same procedure starting with right foot.
3. Do steps to call of "hop, step, close step."
4. Increase rhythm until a fast hop and slow step-close-step is achieved.

253—Pop Goes the Weasel
(Worldtone or Folkcraft 6180)
1. Form double circle, couples facing. One couple facing clockwise, and other counterclockwise.
2. Four skips forward, four skips back.
3. Set of two couples joins hands and skips clockwise once around.
4. First couple lifts joined hands and second couple skips under to move forward to next couple.

254—Pussy Cat
(Worldtone)
1. Children join hands, form circle, all facing center.
2. One or more "Pussy Cats" stand in the center.
3. Children walk counterclockwise around in circle and sing first line.

4. Children walk clockwise as the cat sings second line.
5. Children sing line three as they drop hands, walk toward the cat and shake a finger at him.
6. The cat sings fourth line and jumps on word "chair" frightening others back into circle.
7. Children sing first line of chorus, and take two draw steps (step-close to the side) to right and stamp four times.
8. Repeat procedure while singing second line of chorus.
9. Sing third line of chorus taking four steps forward.
10. Step back three steps while singing line four and jump on last measure.
VERSE:
"Pussy Cat, Pussy Cat, where have you been?
I've been to London to visit the Queen!
Pussy Cat, Pussy Cat, what did you there?
I frightened a mouse from under her chair!''
CHORUS:
Sing "tra, la, la, etc.,'' to same music.

255—Rig-a-Jig-Jig
(Worldtone or Folkcraft 1199)
1. Form circle, all facing center.
2. Select one child to stand in center.
3. Center child walks inside circle.
4. On "a little friend" he stops in front of a partner and bows. (Girls curtsy.)
5. They skip together in circle to the chorus.
6. They split when verse starts and each chooses a new partner.
7. Children in circle may clap to the music.
VERSE:
"As I was walking down the street
Heigh-ho, heigh-ho, heigh-ho, heigh-ho,
A little friend I chanced to meet
Heigh-ho, heigh-ho, heigh-ho.''
CHORUS:
"Rig-a-jig-jig, and away we go,
Away we go, away we go.
Rig-a-jig-jig, and away we go,
Heigh-ho, heigh-ho, heigh-ho.''

256—Right Angle
Tom-tom, suitable rhythm records.
1. Children walk in time to music.
2. On each accented beat or change of music, child moves either right or left at right angle.
3. Must try to change at appropriate times without bumping into other children.

257—Rope Jumping

Records (if music is desired), sash cord, 3/8 to 1/2 inch (rope should come to armpits when person stands on rope with both feet)

1. Place both ends of rope in one hand and turn it on side of body, allowing it to hit the floor lightly on each turn.
2. Jump slightly while turning rope.
3. Coordinate jump and turn of the rope so body is in air when rope slaps floor.
4. After practicing this, assume normal jumping position and apply same technique.
5. After practicing this, routines can be developed.
   a. alternating feet
   b. hopping on one foot
   c. straddle hop — feet together one jump, feet apart on next.
   d. cradle — one foot forward, the other back, one jump forward, the next back
   e. move forward while jumping, skipping, hopping, running
   f. cross hands — cross arms in front while jumping and return on next jump
   g. backward jumping
   h. partner jumping
6. Introduce children to long rope jumping (rope 16-18 feet long).
   a. jump over 6 inches from ground
   b. jump over while it swings
   c. have one child jump while two turn
   d. run, jump, run out
   e. high water
   f. ocean waves
   g. back door
   h. hot pepper
7. Have children jump using two ropes.

258—Schottische-Swedish
(Folkcraft 1411 or choice of good schottische)

1. Form double circle, boys on girls' left, inside hands joined, facing counterclockwise.
2. Begin with outside foot and run forward 3 steps and hop on outside foot.
3. Begin with inside foot, run forward 3 steps and hop on inside foot.
4. Begin with outside foot and take four step-hops, add one of following:
   a. drop hands, turn away, and rejoin.
   b. turn clockwise.

259—Schottische Mixer
(Folkcraft 1471 or any good schottische record)

1. Form double circle, boys on girls' left, inside hands joined, facing counterclockwise.
2. Do basic step (run forward three steps and hop) and repeat.
3. Do four step-hops forward.
4. Repeat step 2.
5. Boy turns in circle on step-hops to move to girl behind him, while each girl turns in place.
6. Repeat steps 2-5 with the new partner.

260—Seven Jumps
(Worldtone or Folkcraft 6172)

1. Form large single circle with hands joined.
2. Do 7 step-hops to right. Jump.
3. Do 7 step-hops to left. Face center.
4. Hands on hips. Lift right knee, stamp right foot. Join hands.
5. Repeat 2-4. Raise left knee, stamp, join hands.
6. Repeat 2-5. Place right elbow on floor, rest chin on right hand. Stand, join hands.
7. Repeat 2-6. Repeat 6 using left elbow and hand. Stand, join hands.
8. Repeat 2-7. Put forehead on floor. Stand, join hands.
9. Repeat 2 and 3.

261—Shoemaker's Dance
(Folkcraft or Worldtone)

1. Form single circle, facing center.
2. "Wind the thread" — revolve fists rapidly around each other in front of the body (forward three times and backward three times).
3. Fingers form the scissors to make cuts on "snip, snap."
4. Pound one fist on other three times for "tap, tap, tap."
5. Repeat steps 2-4.
6. For chorus put on imaginary shoe and skip in circle clockwise. Can pretend to put on shoes of various people.

VERSE:
"See the cobbler wind his thread,
Snip, snap, tap, tap, tap.
That's the way he earns his bread,
Snip, snap, tap, tap, tap."

CHORUS:
"So the cobbler blithe and gay,
Works from morn to close of day,
At his shoes he pegs away,
Whistling cheerily his lay."

262—Shoo, Fly
(Folkcraft record 1102 or Worldtone)

1. Form single circle with boy's partner to his right.
2. Take four steps to center, swinging arms back and forth.
3. Take four steps back, ending with arms outstretched.
4. Repeat steps 2 and 3.
5. Boy swings partner with right elbow and ends with partner on left.
6. Boy turns to girl on right and nods to his new partner.
7. Repeat steps 2-6 with new partner.

VERSE:
"Shoo, fly, don't bother me,
Shoo, fly, don't bother me,
Shoo, fly, don't bother me,
For I belong to somebody.
I do, I do, and I'm not going to tell you who,
For I belong to somebody, yes, indeed I do!"

263—Sicilian Circle
(Folkcraft 1140)

1. Make sets of two couples, one couple facing clockwise and other counterclockwise. Couple's hands joined.
2. Couples take four steps toward each other and back.
3. Couples join hands and circle clockwise.
4. Give right hand to person opposite and pass him, join inside hands and face other couple.
5. Repeat step 4 returning to position.
6. Girls extend right hands to each other, pass, extend left hands to boys who turn them in place.
7. Repeat step 2.
8. Couples walk forward, drop hands, pass through (one girl walking between the two boys).
9. Each couple walks on to meet a new couple after forming new set.

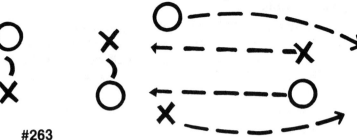

#263

264—Sing a Song of Sixpence
(Worldtone or Folkcraft 1180)

1. Form single circle facing center.
2. Have 6-8 children crouched in center as blackbirds.
3. Sing verse 1:
   a. Walk around in circle.
   b. Take short steps forward with outstretched arms.
   c. Walk back with arms up. Blackbirds "fly" around.
   d. Kneel as if presenting a dish.
4. Sing verse 2:
   a. Pantomime counting money.
   b. Pantomime eating.
   c. Pantomime hanging clothes.
   d. Each blackbird snips off nose of a circle player who becomes a blackbird for the next game.

VERSES:
1. a. "Sing a song of sixpence, a pocket full of rye,
   b. Four and twenty blackbirds, baked in a pie,
   c. When the pie was opened the birds began to sing,
   d. Wasn't that a dainty dish to set before the king?"
2. a. "The king was in his counting house, counting out his money.
   b. The queen was in the pantry, eating bread and honey,
   c. The maid was in the garden, hanging out the clothes,
   d. And down came a blackbird and snipped off her nose!"

265—Spanish Circle
(Folkcraft 1047)

1. Form a circle with sets of two couples, one couple facing clockwise, the other facing counterclockwise. Inside hands joined.
2. Balance forward and back, starting with outside foot, swing arms.
3. Exchange partners with two waltz steps. On first waltz step, swing inside hand forward, release. Boy takes other girl's left hand in his right.
4. Girl turns under his arm and ends beside him. Couples face in and out now.
5. Repeat steps 2-4, and couples are home.
6. All join right hands, do four waltz steps turning clockwise, drop hands. Join left hands, do 4 waltz steps back to position.
7. Boys do side balance and back to place. Repeat. Girls join right hands and balance forward and back. They pass each other, exchange places, turn around to left, back into place.
8. Boys join inside hands with new partner and balance forward and back.
9. Repeat with the exception that sets instead of couples are exchanged.

266—Square Dance Positions

1. Couple with backs to music is #1.
2. Couple to right is #2, etc.
3. "Head couples" are #1 and #3.
4. "Side couples" are #2 and #4.
5. Partner — girl at boy's side.
6. Corner lady — girl to boy's left.
7. Right-hand lady — girl in couple to boy's right.
8. Opposite lady — girl directly across set.
9. Home — starting position.
10. Active or Leading couple — the visiting couple in different figures.

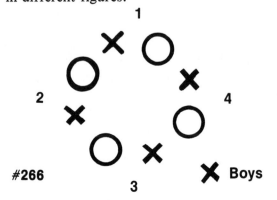

#266

66

267—Tantoli
(Folkcraft R6183)

1. Form double circle, boys on outside facing counterclockwise, inside hands joined, outside hands on hips.
2. Do four heel and toe polka steps.
3. Do two-step three times.
4. Repeat steps 2 and 3.
5. Face partner, join hands, raise arms to shoulder height.
6. Step on one foot and hop, extending other foot to side (boys start on right, girls on left), eight times.
7. Repeat step 6 while turning.

268—Thread Follows the Needle
(Worldtone — Singing Games, Vol. I)

1. Eight children form single line with hands joined. Each child has a number.
2. No. 1 leads others under raised arms of last two children.
3. After all have passed under them, they face other direction, letting arms cross in front of them, forming a stitch.
4. Procedure is repeated until all are members of the stitch.
5. Break the stitch by raising arms over heads and turning back to original position.
6. Can be repeated with new leader.

VERSE:

"The thread follows the needle,
The thread follows the needle,
In and out the needle goes
As mother mends the children's clothes."

269—Three Blind Mice

1. Form square with 6-8 children on each side. Each side acts as one part of a round.
2. Sing song; during line one, clap hands three times.
3. During second line, stamp floor.
4. For line 3, four skips forward.
5. For line 4, four skips back.
6. For line 5, turn in place.
7. For line 6, make cutting motion.
8. For line 7, hands over ears and move head in rocking motion.
9. Clap hands three times for line 8.
10. Sing song twice.

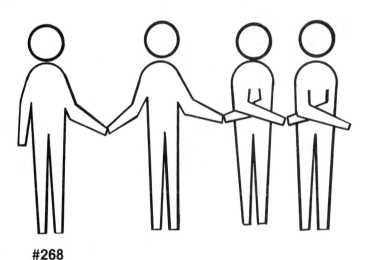

#268

VERSE:

"Three blind mice,
Three blind mice,
See how they run,
See how they run,
They all ran after the farmer's wife
Who cut off their tails with a carving knife
Did you ever see such a sight in your life as
Three blind mice."

270—Twinkle, Twinkle Little Star

1. Form single circle facing center.
2. Take seven tiptoe steps toward center with arms extended overhead and fingers moving.
3. Turn in place using seven tiptoe steps.
4. Each child makes a circle with his arms and moves in a rocking motion.
5. Form diamond with fingers.
6. Repeat step 2, moving backward.
7. Repeat step 3.

VERSE:

"Twinkle, twinkle, little star.
How I wonder what you are.
Up above the world so high
Like a diamond in the sky.
Twinkle, twinkle, little star.
How I wonder what you are."

271—Two Step

1. Basic step — step-close-step.
2. Form double circle with boys on the inside, facing counterclockwise.
3. All move in same direction, starting with outside foot.
4. After practice, have partners face each other, boys start with left foot, girls with right.
5. Develop turn to call of "left, close, pivot" and "right, close, pivot."

#271

272—Varsouvienne
(Folkcraft 1034 or Worldtone)

1. Take varsouvienne position.
   a. Boy holds girl's left hand in front with his left hand.
   b. Girl brings her right hand over her right shoulder.
   c. Boy puts his right arm around her shoulder and grasps her hand.
2. Bend left knee, bring left foot in front of right. Step forward with left, close with right.
3. Repeat step 2.
4. Put left foot over right instep, swing left foot behind right foot taking a step.
5. Step to right with right foot, moving behind girl. Boy steps forward with left (beside girl). Point right toe.
6. Girl does same movements almost in place moving slightly left.
7. Repeat steps 4-6 starting with right foot, remaining in varsouvienne position.
8. Drop right hands. Cross left, step left, step right, step left, point right. Boy steps in place while girl moves left away from boy.
9. Cross right, step right, step left, step right, point left. Girl turns under boy's arm and resumes first position.
10. Repeat steps 8 and 9.

#272

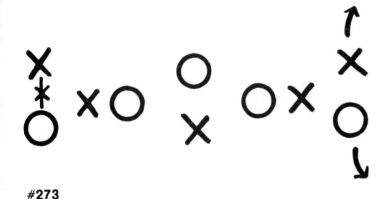

#273

273—Virginia Reel
(Worldtone or Folkcraft 1249 Simplified or 1342)

1. Two parallel facing lines of 6-8 couples, boys on left.
2. All take four steps forward, bow, take four steps back.
3. Partners meet, swing once around with right hands joined, back to place.
4. Repeat step 3 with left hands.
5. Repeat step 3 with both hands.
6. Partners dos-a-dos.
7. Head couple joins hands and slides down the set and back.
8. Head couple swings with right elbows 1½ times, separate, goes to opposite line, swings next person with left elbow and then swings partner.
9. Head couple turns each dancer in order.
10. Reach end, swing around so they are on correct sides, and slide to beginning.
11. At change of music, head boy leads his line around to end, head girl does the same.
12. At foot of set, head couple forms arch. Others skip under arch making a new head couple.
13. Procedure is continued until all couples have been the head couple.

69

274—Waltz

1. Basic step — accented first step (longer), step, close.
2. Clap rhythm accenting first beat.
3. Practice the waltz balance.

275—Yankee Doodle
   (Folkcraft 1080)

1. Form the circle with sets of three (boy with girl on either side) facing counterclockwise.
2. On verse, all march, lifting knees and swinging arms.
3. During first two lines of chorus, boy swings girl to his right with his right hand.
4. On next two lines, he swings girl to his left with his left hand.
5. Boy returns to middle and moves forward to next set.
6. Procedure is repeated.

VERSE:

"Yankee Doodle came to town
Riding on a pony,
Stuck a feather in his hat
And called it macaroni."

CHORUS:

"Yankee Doodle keep it up,
Yankee Doodle dandy;
Mind the music and the step,
And with the girls be handy."

Stunts

276—Arm and Leg Hang

Exercise bar

Hang with one arm and one leg.

277—Back Roller

a. Form human ball by bringing knees up to chest and clasp them with arms.
b. Roll back and forth.
c. Roll forward to a stand.

278—Back-to-Back Push

a. Partners stand back to back between two parallel lines ten feet apart.
b. Try to push each other out of area between lines by pushing backwards against each other.
c. Opponent must not be lifted but pushed out of bounds.

280—Backward Roll

a. Squat down, place hands on mat, shoulder width apart, with fingers pointed forward and knees between arms.
b. Push off with hands quickly, sit down, and start rolling over on the back; at same time bring hands up over shoulders, palms up, fingers pointed backward.
c. Continue rolling backward with knees close to chest.
d. Push hard with hands as they now touch mat at same time as head.
e. Continue rolling over top of head and push off mat until ready to stand.

#278

279—Backward Curl

a. Sit with knees drawn to chest and chin tucked down.
b. Roll backwards until weight is on shoulders with hands placed alongside head on mat to support weight.
c. Feet and legs come back over head with toes touching mat.
d. Roll back to original sitting position.

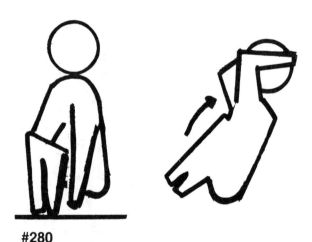

#280

#279

281—Balance Touch
Eraser, block, or rolled-up paper
a. Place object a yard away from a line.
b. Balancing on one foot on line, reach out with other foot, touch object, and return to original position.

283—Bouncer
a. Begin in push-up position. Bounce up and down with both hands and feet leaving ground at same time.
b. Try clapping while doing this.

282—Bear Walk
a. Bend forward touching ground with both hands.
b. Walk slowly forward moving hand and foot on **same side** together.

284—Bouncing Ball
a. Keeping upper body straight, jump up and down from bent-knee position.
b. Start with high bounce and gradually lower height of bounce.
c. Try as partner stunt with one as bouncer and other as ball.

285—Cartwheel
a. Begin with legs and arms spread with left side toward direction of wheeling.
b. Swing left arm up keeping right arm at side.
c. Throw weight to left side, bringing right arm up and left arm down placing left hand two feet from left leg.
d. Place right arm and hand on mat, bringing right leg upward; just before right hand touches mat, push off with left foot.
e. Swing both legs up and over head.
f. Right foot touches first and then left. Give good push with right hand to return to original standing position.
g. Keep head up throughout entire stunt.

#285

286—Catch and Pull Tug-of-War
a. Two teams face each other across a line.
b. Any teammate or chain of players tries to pull any opponent across line.
c. Having been pulled across line, opponent joins other team until time is called.
d. Team capturing most players wins.

287—Centipede
a. Support person gets down on hands and knees while top person faces same direction, placing his hands two feet in front of those of under person.
b. Top person places legs and body on top of support person gripping body of under person with his knees and legs; feet are on top, not hooked under.
c. Couple walks with top person using hands only and support person using both hands and feet; support person does not use knees for support on floor.

288—Chin
Horizontal ladder
With backs of hands facing, grip and raise chin above a rung.

289—Chinese Get-Up
a. Two people sit, back to back, and lock arms.
b. Both stand by pushing against each other's back.
c. Both sit down again, pushing against each other's back.

290—Churn the Butter
a. Partners stand back to back with elbows locked.
b. One partner bends forward from hips while other partner springs from floor lifting his feet up.
c. This movement is alternated between partners.

291—Climbing Scissors Grip
Climbing rope
a. Grab onto rope as high as possible, standing with right leg forward of left leg.
b. Raise left leg, bend at knee and place rope **inside** of knee and **outside** of foot.
c. Cross right leg over left leg and straighten both legs out with toes pointed down.
d. Raise knees up close to chest with rope sliding between them, supporting body with hand grip.
e. Lock rope between legs and climb up with hand-over-hand method.
f. Bring knees up to chest and repeat the process until top mark is reached.

Note: Students must develop strength before attempting to reach top mark.

292—Coffee Grinder
a. Support body on one hand and the feet, with side to floor; keep arm straight and feet slightly apart.
b. Using arm as a pivot, walk completely around arm keeping body and arm straight.
c. Feet walk in a circle.
d. Repeat using other arm.

293—Corkscrew Hang
Horizontal ladder
a. Hang with one hand to a rung.
b. Twist body as far one way as it will go, and then twist it back other way like a corkscrew.

294—Crab Walk
a. Squat down and reach back putting both hands on floor without sitting down.
b. With head, neck, and body level and in a straight line, walk forward, backward, and sideward.

295—Cricket Walk
a. Squat and spread knees.
b. Put arms between knees and grasp outside of ankles with hands.
c. Walk forward and backward, chirping like a cricket.

296—Descending

Climbing rope
a. Reverse scissors climb—from extended position, lock legs and lower body with hands until knees are against chest.
b. Hold with hands and lower legs to new position.

298—Elbow Wrestle

a. Lie on floor or sit at a table facing each other.
b. Clasp right hands with elbows held against each other.
c. Each partner tries to force opponent's arm down while keeping elbows together.
d. Change position using left arms.

299—Elephant Walk

a. Bend forward, clasping hands together forming a trunk.
b. Walk slowly forward with big steps keeping legs straight and swinging trunk from side to side.

300—Eskimo Roll (Double Roll)

a. #1 lies on back, legs raised, knees flexed.
b. #2 stands behind #1's shoulders and reaches forward grasping #1's ankles with fingers to outside, thumbs to inside.
c. #1 grasps #2's ankles in same grip.
d. #2 does forward roll between #1's legs, and pulls to feet.
e. Partners continue to roll changing positions.

297—Dive Forward Roll

a. Take short run and take off with both feet, turning in air as hands come down to cushion fall.
b. Head is tucked under and roll is made on back of neck and shoulders.

#297

301—Finger Touch

a. Place right hand behind back with index finger straight and pointed down.
b. Grasp right wrist with left hand.
c. From erect standing position with feet six inches apart, squat down and touch floor with index finger.
d. Regain erect standing position without losing balance.

#300

#301

302—Fish Hawk Dive

a. Place folded paper on floor with edge up so that it can be picked up with teeth.

b. Kneel on one leg with other leg extended behind and arms out for balance.

c. Lean forward picking up paper with teeth and return to position without losing balance.

303—Flip Flop

a. From push-up position, lift one hand and at same time turn body so back is to floor; return raised hand to floor quickly for support.

b. With weight now on hands and heels, continue with other hand and complete turn.

c. Return by reversing direction and making complete turn back the other way.

304—Forearm Headstand

a. In kneeling position, place both elbows on mat and forepart of head in cupped hands.

b. From this position, support body in an inverted upright position.

c. Spotters are needed.

305—Forward Roll

a. Squat on mat placing hands on mat, shoulder width apart with fingers pointed forward and knees between arms.

b. Push off with feet and rock forward on hands.

c. Just when falling off balance, tuck head down between arms with chin on chest.

d. Back of head touches mat and weight is then born by rounded back.

e. Grasp shins and pull onto feet.

306—Frog Headstand

a. Squat down on mat, placing hands flat, fingers pointing forward, with elbows inside and pressed against inner part of knees.

b. Lean forward using leverage of elbows against knees and balance on hands.

c. Hold for five seconds and return to original position.

307—Frog Jump

a. Squat down with hands placed on floor slightly in front of feet.

b. Jump forward a few feet lighting on hands and feet simultaneously.

308—Front Roll

a. Stand with feet apart facing forward.
b. Squat down and place hands on mat, shoulder width apart.
c. Tuck chin to chest and make a rounded back.
d. Push off, with hands and feet providing force for the roll.
e. Carry weight on rounded back and shoulders, not on head.

309—Gorilla Walk

a. Bend knees slightly and carry trunk forward with arms hanging at side.
b. Walk forward touching fingers to ground at each step.

310—Hand Jumping

Horizontal ladder

a. Jump with both hands at once from one rung to next.
b. Swing body while jumping.

311—Hand Push

a. Stand toe to toe facing opponent.
b. Each opponent places hands in front of his shoulders, palms facing away.
c. Opponents push against each other's hands, trying to force opponent backward to lose balance.
d. Feet must be kept in place.

312—Handstand

a. Place hands on mat, shoulder width apart, fingers spread, slightly cupped and pointed straight ahead.
b. Keeping one leg straight, walk up close with other leg to elevate hips.
c. Keep arms straight and shoulders well forward of hands.
d. Kick up with straight leg and push off with bent leg.
e. With back arched, shoulders are brought back to a point directly over hands.
f. Keep head up, feet together, and toes pointed toward ceiling.
g. Spotters are needed.

#312

313—Hand Wrestle
a. Opponents place right foot against right foot and grasp right hands in handshake grip.
b. Implant left foot firmly to rear for support.
c. Each opponent tries to upset the other by hand and arm pressure to make him move his left foot.

314—Hang from Standing
Climbing rope
Reach up as high as possible, jump to bent-arm position, and hang with feet in following positions:

One or both knees up

Bicycle movement

Half lever

Full lever—bring feet up to face with knees kept straight

315—Head Balance
a. Place beanbag, block, or book on head.
b. Keeping upper body in good posture, walk, stoop, turn around, etc.

316—Headstand
a. Start in squat position with hands pointed forward, fingers spread and slightly cupped, about shoulder width apart.
b. Put head on mat about ten inches from hands, keeping weight on forward part of head (near hairline).
c. Walk feet forward until hips are high over body.
d. Keep one foot on mat and kick other leg up, quickly following with a push by mat foot to bring that leg up to one already in upright position.
e. Keep feet together, legs straight, toes pointed and back arched with weight evenly distributed among hands and head.
f. Return to mat in direction used going up.
g. Spotters are needed.

317—Heel Click — Side

a. Balance on one foot with other out to side.
b. Hop on supporting foot, click heels, and return to balance.
c. Repeat with other foot.

#317

318—Heel Slap

a. Stand in erect position with hands at sides.
b. Jump into air and slap both heels with hands.

#318

319—High Dive

a. Fold piece of paper that can be picked up by teeth.
b. Stand on one foot only, using arms for balance. Try to pick up paper with teeth.

#319

320—Inverted Hang

Climbing rope

a. Jump to bent-arm position.
b. Swing feet up over head and grasp rope between legs holding inverted position with both hands and feet.

#320

321—Jump Hang Position

Climbing rope

a. Jump as high as possible and hang upside down.
b. Repeat all different leg positions from the "hang from standing" stunt.

#321

322—Jumping Jack
a. Squat down with trunk erect.
b. Place one foot ahead of other so that heel of front foot is even with toe of back foot.
c. Place hands palms down on top of head.
d. Spring into air changing relative position of feet.
e. Repeat 5, 10, and 15 times.

324—Jump Stick
a. Hold a three-foot stick by fingers in front of you.
b. Jump over stick by jumping high and passing stick under body.
c. During jump, bring knees up high.

325—Jump Through
a. From push-up position, push off strongly with toes and bring body forward so that hips and legs are extended forward beyond hands and back is to floor.
b. Reverse movement and return to original position.

323—Jumping on Side Rails
Horizontal ladder
a. Place hands on side rails.
b. Make progress forward by moving both hands at once.
c. Also move backwards.

#323

326—King of the Mat
a. All players are on hands and knees on edge of large mat.
b. Each player tries to make another player touch any part of body to floor outside mat.

327—Kip Over
Horizontal ladder
a. Place hands on rails with body facing out.
b. Bring feet up over top of ladder.
c. Return to original position.

#327

328—Knee Dip
a. Grasp right instep behind back with left hand, balancing on left foot.
b. With other arm out for balance, lower and touch floor with bent knee.
c. Regain balance.
d. Repeat with other leg.

329—Knee Jump to Standing
From kneeling position, jump to standing position in one motion.

330—Knee Lift
Horizonal ladder
Hang with knees up so thighs are parallel to ground.

331—Knee and Shoulder Balance
a. Support partner is on back with knees well up and feet flat on floor.
b. He extends hands out to support shoulders of top man.
c. Top man takes position in front of knees and places hands on knees.
d. Top man leans forward so shoulders are supported by hands of bottom man.
e. Top man kicks up to hand and shoulder stand.

#331

82

332—Knee Walk
a. Kneel at end of mat.
b. Reach back and hold both feet up from floor.
c. Walk across mat on knees.
d. Walk forward, backward, and sideward.

333—Lame Dog Walk
a. On all fours, raise one foot in air.
b. Walk as a dog on three legs.

334—Leap Frog
a. Base takes wide stance, bends forward from the hips, and braces hands on knees.
b. Leaper runs forward, places hands on base's shoulders and vaults, extending legs to side.
c. Land on both feet, knees and ankles relaxed.

335—Leg Balance
a. Forward: with knee straight, extend leg forward with toe pointed, holding position five seconds, using arms out to side for balance.
b. Backward: extend leg backward parallel to floor, eyes forward, arms out to side for balance, hold five seconds without moving.

336—Leg Dip
a. Extend hands and one leg forward while balancing on other leg.
b. Lower body to heel seat. Rise without losing balance or touching anything.
c. Try with other foot.

#336

337—Long Reach
Piece of chalk
a. Keep toes behind a line and with a piece of chalk, reach out as far as possible, balancing weight on feet and one hand.
b. Make a mark with the chalk and recover without touching the supporting hand a second time.

338—Long Vault
a. Review leap frog.
b. In Long Vault there are two children down forming a longer back.
c. The child clears both children with one vault.
d. Two spotters are needed standing alongside the forward back.

339—Lowering the Boom

a. Start from a push-up position. Lower the body completely to the ground by use of the arms only.

b. The body remains straight.

#339

340—Measuring Worm

a. From a front-leaning position, keeping knees stiff, inch forward with feet and bring them up as close as possible to the hands.

b. Regain position by inching hands forward.

341—Mule Kick

a. Bend forward and place hands on floor.

b. Bend knees and kick into air as a mule.

342—Partner Hopping

a. Children hop together a short distance.

b. Three combinations are suggested:

   1. Stand facing each other. Hop on right leg and extend left leg forward to be grasped by the partner.

   2. Stand back to back with the knee bent and leg grasped by the partner. Hop as before.

   3. Partners stand side by side with inside arms around each other's waist. Hop forward on outside foot.

343—Partners on Balance Beam

Balance beam

a. Walk forward, inside hands joined. Walk backward.

b. Walk sideward with both hands joined.

c. Walk sideward with both hands joined using grapevine step (alternate crossing feet behind and in front while stepping).

#341

84

344—Pencil

Horizontal ladder

Hang from a rung with feet pointed to ground.

345—Pogo Stick

a. Pretend to be a pogo stick by keeping a stiff body and jumping on the toes.
b. Hold hands in front as if grasping a stick.
c. Progress in various directions.

346—Pull-Ups and Return on Hanging Rope

a. Use hand-over-hand grips.
b. Pull up from lying position to sitting.
c. Pull up from sitting to standing.
d. Pull up from lying position to standing, keeping straight.

347—Puppy Dog Run

a. Place hands on floor, keeping head up, and bending arms and legs slightly.
b. Walk and run like a happy puppy.

348—Push-Ups

a. Get on hands and knees with hands shoulder distance apart.
b. Extend legs backward until hips and knees are straight.
c. Lower body, by bending elbows until nose touches floor.
d. Raise body and repeat.

349—Rabbit Jump

a. Place hands on the floor in front of the feet; get into a knee bend position, with the knees pointed out.
b. Move forward with hands first and then bring the feet up to the hands.

350—Rising Sun

a. Lie on back.
b. Rise to a standing position using the arms only for balance.

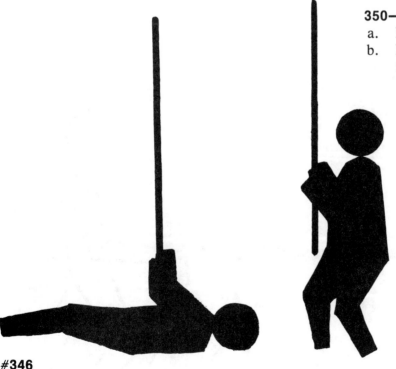

#346

351—Rocking Horse

a. Face down on a mat.
b. Reach back with hands, grasping the insteps with hands.
c. With the back arched, rock back and forth.

352—Rolling Log

a. Lie on back with arms extended over head, legs straight. Roll slowly over to end of mat.
b. The body must move as "one piece" to keep direction straight.

353—Rooster Fight

a. Couple face with arms folded across chest and weight on one foot.
b. On signal each tries to throw the other off balance by pushing with his arms.
c. First one to lose balance by putting down a foot, loses.

354—Rope Tug-of-War

One rope and a piece of tape

a. Two equal teams face each other on opposite ends of a rope.
b. A piece of tape marks the center of the rope.
c. Two parallel lines are drawn about 10 feet apart.
d. At the start, the center marker is midway between the lines.
e. Each team tries to pull the center marker over its near line.

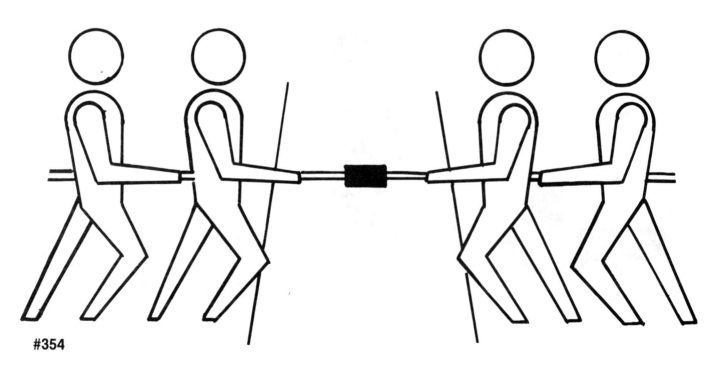

#354

355—Russian Dance
a. Squat on one heel while other leg is halfway to the side, with knee straight and resting on heel.
b. Fold arms in front and hold high.
c. Change feet rapidly.

#355

356—Scissors
Horizontal ladder
a. Hang with the feet pointed and moving back and forth like scissors.
b. Move legs from side, crossing each time.

357—Scooter
a. Sit on the floor with feet extended in front.
b. Hold body erect and arms crossed about the level of the chin.
c. To scoot, lift seat and move it forward toward heels.
d. Extend legs again.

358—Seal Crawl
a. Start from push-up position with fingers turned to side as flappers.
b. Keep legs together, weight on toes.
c. Drag body along by walking on hands and let hips swing.

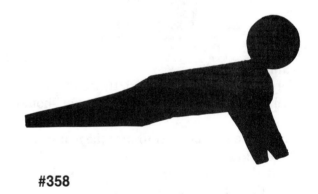

#358

359—Seat Balance
a. Sit on floor, holding ankles in front with elbows inside the knees.
b. The feet are flat on the floor, and the knees are bent at a right angle.
c. Raise legs so that the knees are straight with the toes pointed and balance on seat for 5 seconds.

#359

360—Side Roll

a. Start on hands and knees with the side selected for the roll toward the direction of the roll.

b. Drop the shoulder and tuck the elbow and knee under, roll over on the shoulders and hips, coming again to the hands and knees position.

361—Sit-Ups

a. Lie flat on floor with arms folded on chest, legs near buttocks, bent with feet on floor.

b. Come to sitting position. Touch arms to thighs.

c. Lie down slowly. (Partner holds feet to floor.)

#361

362—Shoulder Roll

a. For a shoulder roll to the left, stand with feet well apart and the left arm extended at shoulder height.

b. Throw the left shoulder toward the mat in a rolling motion.

c. With the left forearm and elbow touching the mat, the roll is made on the shoulder and upper part of the back.

d. The finish is up on the knee and then back to the standing position.

#362

363—Shoulder Shove
a. Start on one foot with the other foot held by the opposite hand.
b. Each contestant tries to knock or bump the other off balance so that he will let go of his leg.

#363

#364

364—Skin the Cat
Horizontal ladder
a. Hang from a rung and bring the knees up to the chest.
b. Continue to thrust the legs and feet over the head until they again point toward the ground.
c. Return to original position.

365—Sloth Travel
Horizontal ladder
a. Hang by hands and feet.
b. Travel along the bar like a sloth.

#365

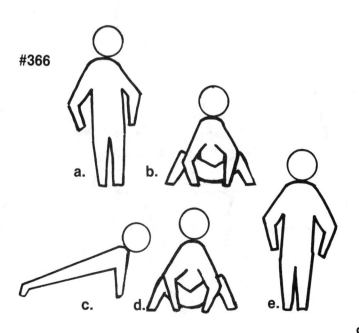

#366

366—Squat Thrust
a. Start from the position of attention.
b. On the count of one, squat down on the floor, placing hands flat on the floor with the elbows inside the knees.
c. On the count of two, the feet and legs are thrust back so that the body is perfectly straight from head to toe, in push-up position.
d. On the count of three, return to squat position.
e. On the count of four, return to the position of attention.

367—Step on Toes
a. Face opponent.
b. The object is to step on the other's toes.

369—Stunt-Type Beam Activities
Balance beam
a. Use various walks, balancing an object on the head.
b. Walk to the center, perform a stunt, and continue to end.
c. Stunts to be used include kneeling, touching the floor, walking under a wand, stepping over a wand.

370—Tandem Bicycle
a. This stunt can be performed by two or more players.
b. The first player forms a bicycle by bending his knees.
c. The second player sits lightly on first player's knees.
d. Other players may be added in the same fashion.
e. The hands are on the hips of the person in front for support.
f. Progress by moving the feet on the same side together.

368—Stoop and Stretch
Two pieces of chalk
a. Hold a piece of chalk in both hands.
b. Place the heels against a line, feet about a foot apart.
c. Reach between legs with knees straight and make a mark as far back as you can.

#369

#370

90

371—Three Point Tip-Up
a. Squat down, placing hands flat with fingers pointing forward and elbows inside pressed against the inner part of the knees.
b. Lean forward, transferring weight onto the elbows and hands until forehead touches the mat.
c. Return to position.

#371

372—Tightrope Walk
a. Walk a line drawn on the floor.
b. Use arms for balance.
c. Pretend to jump rope, juggle balls, ride a bicycle, etc.

373—Toe Touch Nose
a. From a sitting position, use hands to touch the nose with the toe of either foot.
b. Do first with one foot and then with the other foot.

374—Toe Tug Walk
a. Bend over and grasp the toes, keeping the thumb on top.
b. Keep eyes forward and knees slightly bent.
c. Walk in various ways without losing the grip on the toes.

375—Top
a. From a standing position with arms at the side, jump and twist to face the opposite direction.
b. Twist three-quarters of the way around, and make a full twist facing the original direction.
c. Successful execution of stunt calls for landing with good balance with hands near the sides.

376—Travels
Horizontal ladder
a. Move forward using every other rung.
b. Try using every third rung.

377—Tug-of-War
a. Opponents face each other across a line with right (or left) hands clasped in a wrist grip.
b. The object is to pull the opponent across the line.

378—Turk Stand

a. Stand with feet apart and arms folded in front.
b. Pivot on the balls of the feet and face the opposite direction.
c. The legs are now crossed.
d. Sit in this position.
e. Reverse this process.
f. Rise without the aid of the hands and uncross the legs with a pivot to face the original direction.

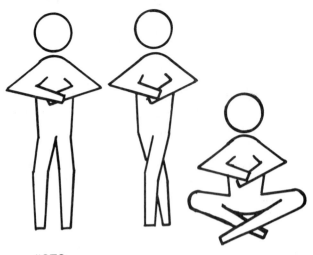

#378

379—Twister

a. Partners face and grasp right hands in a handshake grip.
b. #1 swings his right leg over the head of the other and turns around taking a straddle position over his own arm.
c. #2 swings his left leg over the partner who is bent over, and the partners are now back to back.
d. #1 now continues with his left leg and faces in the original direction.
e. #2 swings his right leg over back to the original face-to-face position.

380—Squat Jumps

a. Take a ¾ squat position with the trunk erect and one foot slightly ahead of the other so that the heel of the front foot is even with the toe of the back.
b. Hands are placed palms down on top of the head.
c. Spring into the air and change the relative position of the feet.
d. Make 5, 10, and 15 changes, clearing the floor by 4 inches.
e. Children should avoid going down to a full squat position.

381—Walking on a Single Beam

Balance beam

a. Walk forward and backward with arms at different positions.
b. Side-step with hands in various positions.
c. Walk forward, backward, using follow steps.
d. Move halfway across beam with one step; complete the trip with another step.

382—Walrus Walk
a. Begin with a front leaning rest position.
b. Make progress by moving both hands forward at the same time.

#382

383—Wand Catch
A wand
a. Stand a wand on one end and hold it in place with the index finger on top.
b. Bring the foot quickly over the stick, letting go and catching the stick before it falls.
c. Do this right and left, inward and outward.

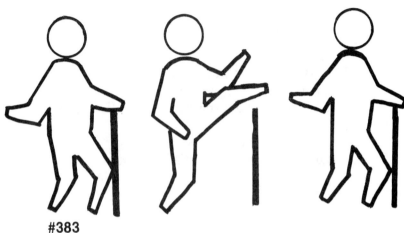

#383

384—Wicket Walk
a. With knees straight, bend forward touching floor with hands.
b. Walk forward and backward with small steps, keeping legs and arms close together.

#384

385—Wrestler's Bridge
a. Lie on the mat, bringing up the feet so that they are flat on the mat.
b. Push up with the body and arch the neck so that the support is on the feet and head.

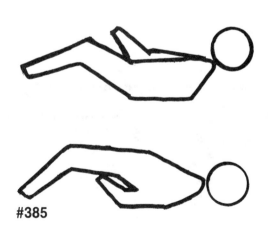

#385

386—Wring the Dishrag
a. Partners face and join hands.
b. Raise one pair of arms and turn under that pair of arms.
c. Stand back to back.
d. Raise other pair of arms and turn under.

#386

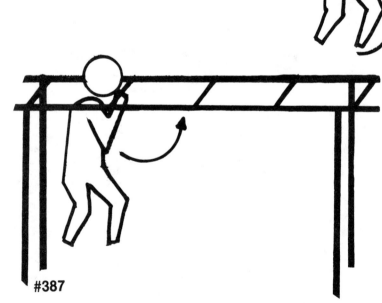

#387

387—Jump and Chin
a. Begin on first rung and raise chin over rung.
b. Jump to next rung and repeat down the ladder.

388—Monkey Crawl
a. Travel underneath the bar with hands and feet.
b. Move forward and backward.

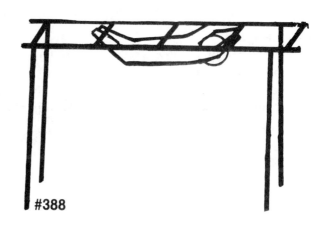

#388

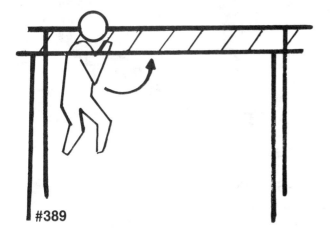

#389

389—Travels
a. Move forward using every other rung.
b. Try using every third rung.

390—Climbing
a. Hand-over-hand method is performed by reaching up high and grasping rope.
b. Raise knees up with rope sliding between them.
c. Lock rope between legs and climb up using hand over hand. Repeat process.

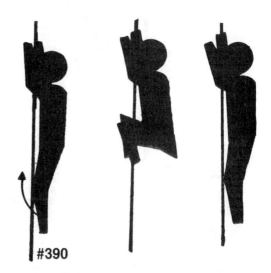

#390

391—Descending
a. Use hand-over-hand method in reverse order.
b. Use legs, with rope between them, to slow fall.

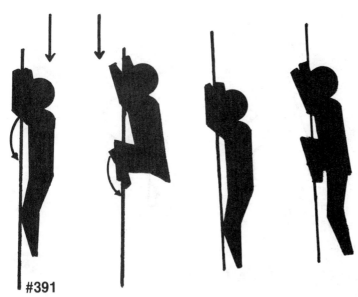

#391

392—Grip
a. Reach as high as possible on the rope.
b. Raise the right leg and place the rope **inside** of the knee and **outside** the foot.
c. Cross the left leg over the right leg. This should give a secure hold.

#392

393—Hanging
a. Grasp rope high above head; hang; pull up until elbows are bent and lower body to floor.
b. From a bent-arm position, bring the body over the head, continuing the body roll until feet touch mat.

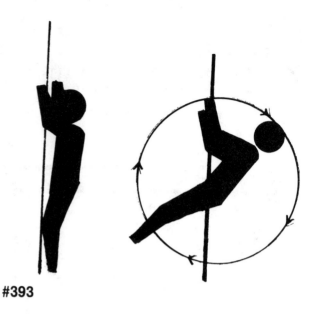

#393

394—Swinging
Shift body weight to achieve pendulum action.

#394

395—Dive Forward Roll
a. Child should take a short run and take off with both feet so that he is partially turning already in the air as his hands come down to cushion the fall.
b. The head is tucked under and the roll is made on the back of the neck and shoulders.

#395

#396

396—Hawk Fish Dive
a. Kneel on one knee with the other leg entirely off the ground.
b. Bend forward and touch nose to floor directly in front of bended knee.

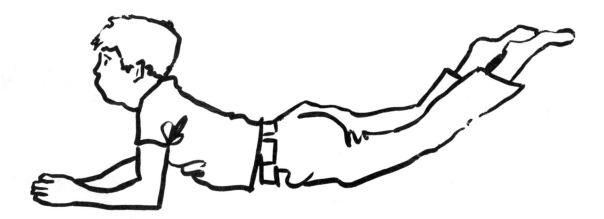

397—Forearm Headstand
a. Take a kneeling position, both elbows on the mat and the forepart of the head in the cupped hands.
b. Support the body in an introverted upright position.
c. Spotters are needed.

398—Reclining Pull-Ups
a. One pupil lies on back. His partner stands astride him, looking face to face, with his feet alongside the reclining child's chest.
b. Partners grasp hands with fingers interlocked.
c. Pupil on floor pulls up with arms until his chest touches partner's thighs. His body remains straight, with the weight resting on the heels.
d. Return to position.

#398

399—Scooter
a. Sit on floor with feet extended, body erect, and arms high, crossed about chin level.
b. To scoot, lift seat and move forward toward heels.
c. Extend legs again; repeat process.

400—Modified Wrestler's Bridge
a. Lie on the back.
b. Place the hands alongside the buttocks, palms down.
c. Lift the body from the floor so that only the heels, hands, and head touch.
d. If the hands are placed out to the sides, a more demanding exercise can be given.

#399

#400

401—Sitting Balance

a. The under, or support, person lies on his back with arms out to the side for support. He keeps his feet in a position as if pushing up the ceiling.

b. He bends his knees and the partner sits on the soles of his feet.

c. Partner is balanced in sitting position with arms out for balance and feet extended forward with toes pointed.

d. Be sure a spotter is stationed behind the pair so the top man does not go over backwards.

#401

402—King of the Mat

a. Players start with hands on knees at edge of mat.

b. Players try to make opponents touch an area outside the mat.

403—Stick Wrestle

a. Two players hold stick between them.

b. Each player tries to get the other to lose his grip.

404—Chinese Pull-Up

a. Opponents sit facing each other with their heels on the floor and toes touching.

b. The object is to pull each other up.

#404

98

405—Peg Pickup
a. Two players grasp rope with a loop at each end.
b. A peg is placed behind each player.
c. Object is to pick up the peg first while holding the rope.

406—Rope Tug-of-War
a. Team at each end pulls in opposite directions.
b. Team loses if pulled across middle line.

#405

407—Rooster Fight
a. Players grasp hands behind knees and stoop.
b. The one who can upset the other players wins.

408—Bulldog
a. Players put hands on knees and face each other.
b. A loop is placed over necks of the players.
c. Object is to pull your opponent over the middle line.

#408

409—Back-to-Back Push
a. Teams are back-to-back in parallel lines.
b. Lock elbows and lower bodies.
c. Try to push opponent out of area.

#409

410—Catch and Pull Tug-of-War
a. Two teams face each other.
b. Each player tries to pull an opponent across the line.
c. Team capturing the most players is the winner.

411—Fitness Tests
Youth Fitness Council (Kennedy Program)
a. Pull-ups (modified for girls)
b. Sit-ups
c. Shuttle run
d. Standing broad jump
e. Fifty-yard dash.
f. Softball throw for distance
g. 600-yard run—walk
   Use Kennedy Blue Book.

413—Balance Beam Exercises
a. Hold arms behind back, walk to the middle, and return.
b. Walk to middle, pick up eraser, and return.
c. Walk backward with eraser on head, turn around, and return.
d. Walk to middle, do a support, and return.
e. Do a balance stand with arms outstretched and body horizontal.
f. Hold stick over beam and step over it with eraser balanced on head.
g. Walk to middle, pick up object with teeth, and return.
h. Walk on beam different ways with eyes closed.
i. Record time standing on beam with eyes closed.
j. Two people walk to middle and pass each other.
k. Do the wheelbarrow with a partner holding up your feet.
l. "Cat Walk" forward and backward on the beam.

412—Pull-Up
a. Grasp bar and pull yourself up to chin level.
b. Repeat.

#412

100

Relays

414—Arch Ball Relay

Ball for each team
a. Head player hands ball over head to next player.
b. End player receives ball, runs to head of line, passes ball back again.
c. When original head returns, race is over.

#414

416—Bounce Ball Relay

Bouncing balls
a. Draw circle 10-15 feet in front of each team.
b. First player goes to circle, bounces ball once, and returns ball to second player who repeats the same routine.
c. Last man in team to carry ball over finish line wins.

417—Beanbag Pass Relay

Beanbag for each team
a. Players stand in lane.
b. Player on right starts beanbag.
c. Race is over when it gets to end of line.

415—Attention Relay

a. Two teams face each other 10 feet apart.
b. Mark two turning points, one 10 feet in front and the other 10 feet behind.
c. Players are numbered from front to rear.
d. Teacher calls attention, and calls a number.
e. Player with number runs around front and back marker.
f. First team to have all at attention wins point.

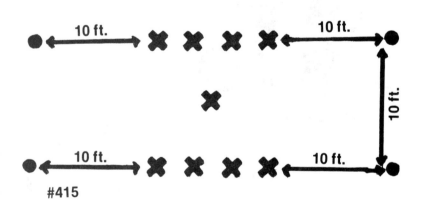

#415

#417

418—Bear Walk Relay

a. Touch ground with both hands while bending forward.
b. Move hand and foot on the same side together.
c. One player at a time walks like a bear to a turning point and back.
d. The first team to have all players back in original starting position wins.

#418

419—Bowl Relay

Ball for each team

a. Head player for each team has a ball.
b. Draw a 15 to 20-foot line in front of each team.
c. First player runs to line, turns, and rolls ball to second player.
d. Second player waits behind starting line to catch ball and repeats pattern.
e. When last player receives ball and carries it over forward line, the race is over.

420—Carry and Fetch Relay

Beanbag for each team

a. First runner carries bag to circle, runs back and tags off.
b. This pattern continues until each player has either fetched or carried bag.

421—Circle Pass Relay

Ball for each team

a. Each team forms small separate circle.
b. Leader passes ball around circle.
c. When ball gets back to leader, whole team sits down.
d. First team to sit in good formation wins.

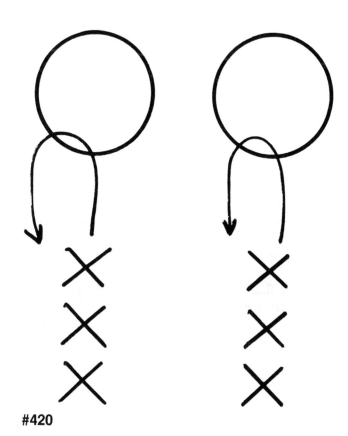

#420

422—Crab Walk Relay

a. Squat down and reach back putting both hands on the floor without sitting down.

b. With head, neck, and body level and in a straight line, walk forward to a turning point and back.

c. The first team to have all players back in original starting position wins.

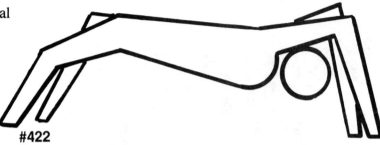

#422

#423

423—Cricket Walk Relay

a. Squat and spread knees.

b. Put arms between knees and grasp the outside of ankles with hands.

c. Walk forward to a turning point and back.

d. The first team to have all players back in original starting position wins.

424—Elephant Walk Relay

a. Form trunk by clasping hands together.

b. Slowly walk forward, legs straight, swinging trunk.

c. One player at a time walks like an elephant to a turning point and back.

d. The first team to have all players back in original starting position wins.

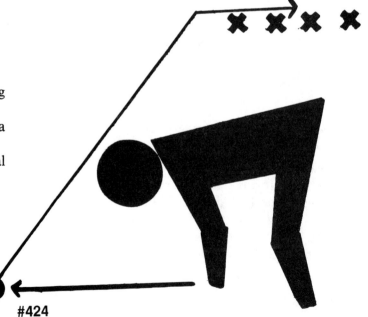

#424

425—Five-in-a-Row Relay

Beanbags or blocks

a. Front player of each team hops forward and places five objects one at a time reasonably spaced, with the last object placed over a line drawn 20 feet in front of teams.

b. He changes hopping foot and returns, hopping over each object.

c. Second player hops forward over each object until he reaches the farthest one.

d. He changes his hopping foot and hops back, picking up the blocks one at a time.

e. He hands the blocks to the third player who puts out the blocks.

f. Each player in turn either distributes or gathers the blocks.

426—Frog Jump Relay

a. From a squatting position, with the hands placed on the floor slightly in front of the feet, jump forward a few feet lighting on the hands and feet simultaneously.

b. Continue this until a turning point is reached and return.

c. The first team to have all players back in original starting position wins.

427—Galloping Relay

a. One player at a time gallops to a turning point and returns.

b. The first team to have all players back in original starting position wins.

428—Gorilla Walk Relay

a. Bend knees slightly and carry the trunk forward. Arms hang at the side.

b. Touch fingers to the ground at each step.

c. Continue this until a turning point is reached and return.

d. The first team to have all players back in original starting position wins.

429—Shuttle Relays
a. Fundamental Movements: running forward or backward, hopping forward or backward.
b. Stunt Movements: Puppy Dog Run, Rabbit Jump, Crab.
c. Simple soccer skills, particularly dribbling.
d. Variety Movements: walking on heels, walking heel and toe, alternate double gallops, etc.

430—Hopping Relay
a. One player at a time hops to a turning point and back.
b. The first team to have all players back in original starting position wins.

431—Jumping Relay
a. One player at a time jumps to a turning point and back.
b. The first team to have all players back in original starting position wins.

432—Lame Dog Walk Relay
a. Walk on both hands and one foot.
b. The other foot is held in the air as if injured.
c. Walk to a starting position, change feet, and return.
d. The first team to have all players back in original starting position wins.

433—Head Balance Relay
Beanbag, block or book
a. Place book, block, etc., on head.
b. One player at a time walks with object on head to turning point and back.
c. The first team to have all players back in original starting position wins.

434—Measuring Worm Relay
a. From a front leaning position, keeping knees stiff, bring the feet as close as possible to hands by inching forward with the feet.
b. Regain position by inching the hands forward.
c. Continue this until a turning point is reached and return.
d. The first team to have all players back in original starting position wins.

435—Pogo Stick Relay
a. Pretend to be a pogo stick by keeping a stiff body and jumping on the toes.
b. Hold the hands in front as if grasping the stick.
c. Continue this until a turning point is reached and return.
d. The first team to have all players back in original starting position wins.

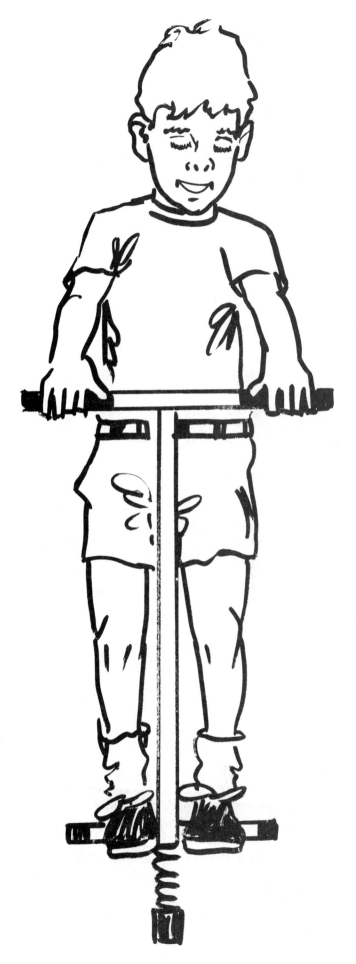

436—Puppy Dog Run Relay
a. Place hands on floor.
b. Bend arms and legs slightly.
c. One player at a time runs like a puppy to a turning point and back.
d. The first team to have all players back in original starting position wins.

#436

437—Rabbit Jump Relay
a. Place hands on floor in front of feet with knees pointed out.
b. Go forward first with hands, then bring feet up to hands.
c. One player at a time jumps like a rabbit to a turning point and back.
d. The first team to have all players back in original starting position wins.

#437

438—Rolling Log Relay
a. Lie on back with arms stretched overhead.
b. Roll sideways the length of the mat.
c. Next time roll with hands pointed toward the other side of the mat.
d. To roll in a straight line keep the feet slightly apart.
e. Roll to a starting position and back.
f. The first team to have all players back in original starting position wins.

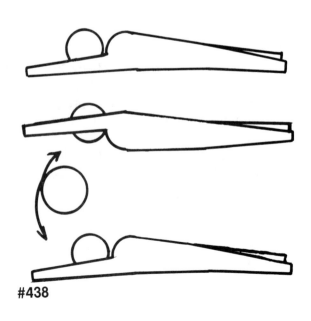

#438

439—Running Relay

a. One player at a time runs to a turning point and back.

b. The first team to have all players back in original starting position wins.

440—Run Up, Walk Back Relay

a. One player at a time runs up to a starting point and walks back.

b. The first team to have all players back in original starting position wins.

#441

441—Seal Crawl Relay

a. Child is in a front leaning (push-up) position, the weight supported on straightened arms and toes.

b. Keeping the body straight, the child walks forward using his hands for propelling force and dragging his feet.

c. Continue this until a turning point is reached and return.

d. The first team to have all players back in original starting position wins.

442—Skipping Relay

a. One player at a time skips to a turning point and back.

b. The first team to have all players back in original starting position wins.

443—Sliding Relay

a. One player at a time slides to a turning point and back.

b. The first team to have all players back in original starting position wins.

444—Tightrope Walk Relay

a. Make a straight line with chalk.

b. Hold arms out for balance.

c. One player at a time walks while balancing himself on line to a turning point and back.

d. The first team to have all players back in original starting position wins.

445—Walking Relay

a. One player at a time walks to a turning point and back.

b. The first team to have all players back in original starting position wins.

446—Corner Fly Relay

Two balls

a. Players are in line facing leader who has a ball.

b. Leader passes ball to and receives from each player beginning with player on his left.

c. When last player on his right receives ball, this player calls out "Corner fly," runs forward and takes spot as the leader, who takes a place in the line to his left.

d. All players adjust position moving over one place to fill spot vacated by new leader.

e. Each player becomes leader, and when original leader returns to his spot with ball, relay is over.

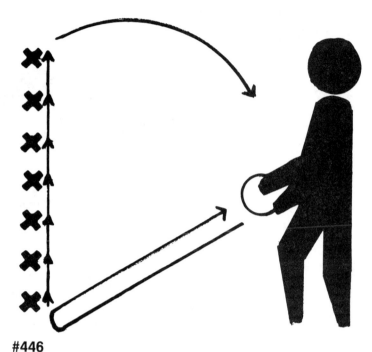

447—Figure Eight Dribbling Basketball Relay

Two basketballs, six Indian clubs

#446

a. Three Indian clubs are placed in a line about five yards apart and five yards in front of each team.

b. First player must run up to clubs and dribble in and out of them in path of a figure eight.

c. Player then runs back and gives ball to second player who repeats process.

d. First team back to original position wins.

448—Around the Bases

Four bases

a. One team lines up at second base, and the other team lines up at home plate.

b. The lead-off player circles the four bases, followed by each player in turn.

c. Side finishing first wins.

d. Fouls: running over three feet outside base line; failure to touch each base.

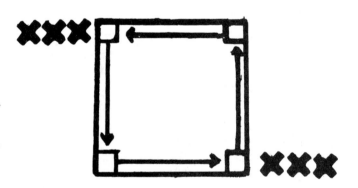

#448

110

449—Indian Club
Six clubs
a. Three Indian clubs are set in small circle 20 feet in front of each team.
b. First player runs and knocks clubs down, second player runs and stands clubs up, one at a time.
c. First team back to starting position wins.

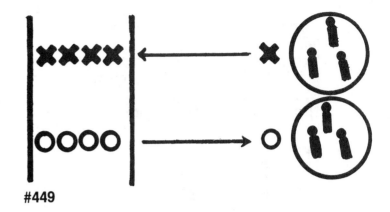

#449

450—Chariot Relay
a. Two lines are drawn 40 feet apart with two teams divided into groups of three standing behind one line.
b. Two people form a "chariot" by standing side by side with inside hands joined.
c. The "driver" stands behind and grasps the outside hands of the "chariot."
d. The chariot runs to one line and back, tagging the next chariot, which repeats the performance.

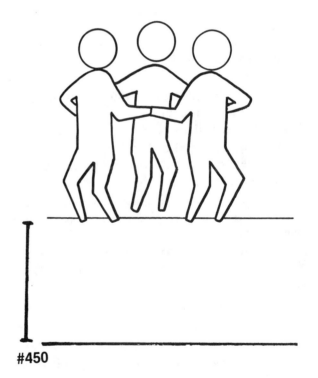

#450

451—Circle Dribbling Relay
Two basketballs
a. Two teams each form large circle standing three yards apart and facing in.
b. One player starts dribbling ball around circle weaving in and out between players.
c. After player completes circle he passes to player ahead of him who repeats performance.

452—Figure Eight Dribbling Soccer Relay

Two soccer balls, six Indian clubs

a. Three Indian clubs stand in line, four yards apart with the first club four yards from starting line.

b. First player dribbles up to first club and then dribbles in and out of each, forming a figure eight.

c. He finishes by dribbling ball or kicking it back to starting line, where second player repeats process.

d. First team back to original position wins.

#452

454—Pass and Squat Relay

Two balls

a. No. 1 has ball and stands about 10 feet in front of his team, which is in a line.

b. No. 1 passes ball to No. 2, who squats down after he has returned ball to No. 1.

c. No. 1 then passes ball to No. 3, who squats down and returns ball to No. 1, and so on.

d. The last man to receive ball straddles members of his team, including No. 1, who has taken a place at head of line.

e. The last man then becomes passer and receiver.

f. When original No. 1 is back to passing position, game is over.

#454

453—Lane Relays

a. Teams are in lane formation. Lanes are 10-15 feet apart.

b. First player runs forward, around turning point, and back to his team.

c. He repeats the trip with second player in tow.

d. Process is repeated until the entire team runs around the turning point and returns to the starting line.

#453

455—Pony Express

a. Two lines are drawn 20-30 feet apart.

b. After each team selects a rider, the players number off with the even numbers on one side and the odd on the other.

c. On signal the rider mounts back of No. 1 who carries him to No. 2. The rider, without touching the ground, exchanges mounts and No. 2 carries him to No. 3, and so on.

d. If rider falls, he must mount again at the place of fall.

e. If he falls in changing mounts, he must get on original mount before making change.

#455

456—Potato Relay

Two small boxes, eight blocks, or beanbags

a. A small box is placed five feet in front of each lane.
b. Four 12-inch circles are drawn five feet beyond the box.
c. Four blocks are placed in each box.
d. First player takes one block and puts it in first circle, returns for second block and puts it in second circle and so on.
e. When four blocks are in circles, first player tags second player, who brings back the blocks one at a time to the box. He tags the third player, who returns blocks to circles, and so on.

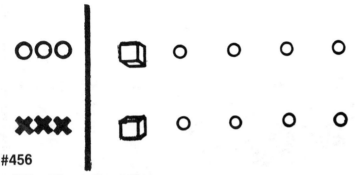

#456

459—Three-Spot Relay

a. Three parallel lines are drawn in front of teams at distances of 10, 20, and 30 feet. These lines provide three spots for each team.
b. Each player is given three tasks to perform, one at each spot.
c. He then runs back and tags off next player who repeats performance.
d. Suggested tasks:
   Prone (face down on floor)
   Back (lie on back on floor)
   Obeisance (touch forehead to floor)
   Nose and toe (touch nose to toe from sitting position)
   Do a specified number of hops, jumps, push-ups, sit-ups, etc.
   Perform designated stunt like Coffee Grinder, Knee Dip, etc.

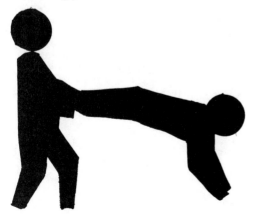

#460

457—Shuttle Relays

a. No. 1 runs to opposite line and touches No. 2 and goes to foot of line.
b. No. 2 runs, and so forth.
c. All runners end up on opposite sides.

458—Stride Ball

Volleyball or soccer ball for each team

a. Teams stand in deep-stride position and pass or roll ball between legs to the back of line.
b. Last player in line carries the ball to the head of the line and starts ball again through legs.
c. First team back to starting position wins.

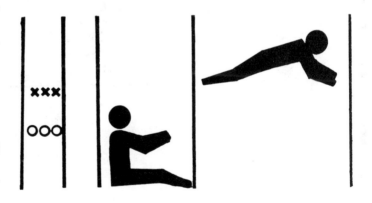

#459

460—Wheelbarrow Relay

a. Divide teams into pairs.
b. One person walks on his hands while partner holds him by knees, wheeling him down to a mark.
c. Change positions for return.
d. First pair tags off second pair, and so on.

Athletic Skills

BASKETBALL SKILLS

462—Hook Pass

1. A step is made with the left foot. The right foot is swung around to the left with a jump and left turn of the body. While in the air a whip is made with the right arm almost straight over the right shoulder near the head.
2. When the ball is released, the elbow is slightly bent and the waist and finger turned down to bring the ball down to the receiver's easiest reach.
3. Body should be facing the direction of the pass upon completion.
4. Left-handed players reverse the movements.

PASSING

#462

#463

463—Baseball Pass

1. Stand with body as in throwing a baseball: perpendicular to receiver and ball held over shoulder with both hands.
2. Have good form for best accuracy.

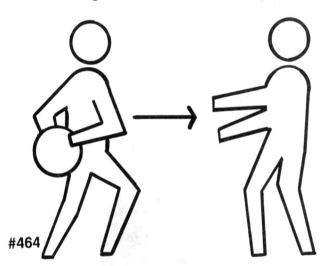

#464

464—Two-Hand Underhand Pass

1. Place hands at side of ball with fingers well spread, gripping only with cushions of fingers and just enough firmness to control ball and allow freedom of movement.
2. Carry ball back to hips, moving one arm back and the other across the body, and pass.

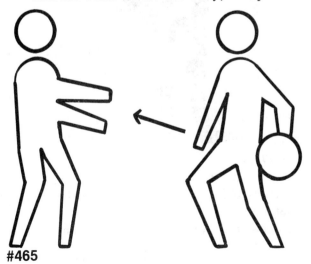

#465

465—One-Hand Underhand Pass

1. Ball held same as for two-hand pass until time of delivery.
2. When passing, one hand is underneath and slightly back of the ball.
3. There is a decided wrist snap when the ball is passed to give momentum and direction to the ball.

466—Bounce Pass

1. The ball is passed using a wrist snap or push.
2. The ball is bounced so that the receiver catches it on first bounce.

467—Chest Pass

1. Hold ball in cushions of fingers in front of chest.
2. Place hands slightly in back of ball.
3. Release with a vigorous snap of the wrist and fingers.
4. When releasing, step forward with one foot, bringing the other foot forward upon release.
5. Keep elbows close to body.

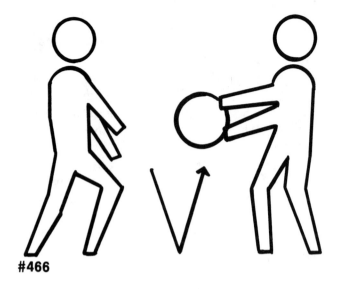

#466

468—Catching

1. Keep the eye on the ball.
2. Catch the ball at waist or near shoulder height.
3. Catch ball close to body, fingers spread and pointed down or up, elbows bent, wrist pliable.
4. Be relaxed, give with ball.
5. Tighten grip on ball after it strikes broad surface of hand.

469—Chest Push Shot

1. Hold ball chest high, with feet in normal stance, one foot slightly ahead.
2. Hold hands behind ball, rotating them inward during the push (push then becomes natural).
3. Have good follow-through.

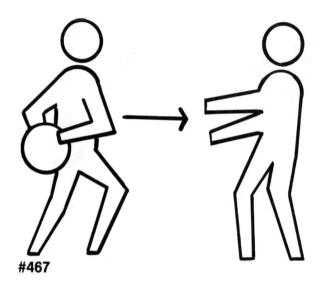

#467

SHOOTING

#469

470—Lay-Up

1. Carry ball in both hands, until shot is made, pushing off with opposite foot of the shooting hand.
2. Extend arm fully during jump and aim at target.
3. Keep hand behind ball during shot.

#470

116

471—One-Hand Set
1. Hold ball in front of shooting arm shoulder, holding ball on opposite hand.
2. Have good wrist action in push, aiming to clear hoop.

#471

472—One-Hand Jump
1. Hold ball over head, shooting hand placed behind ball and under it.
2. Jump off both feet and shoot at apex of jump, using good wrist action.

#472

PIVOTING

#473

473—Front Pivot
1. Keep foot nearest sideline anchored.
2. Rotate inner leg forward and across the outer leg.

#474

474—Rear Pivot (when opponent is in front of player)
1. If left turn is desired, anchor right foot and bring left foot across and around right leg.
2. This brings the back to guard.
3. Opposite for right turn.

475—Guarding

1. Keep knees slightly bent and feet at comfortable stance.
2. Keep 2-3 feet from opponent and be relaxed.
3. Keep one hand in opponent's line of vision, sliding with his moves.

#475

#476

476—Dribbling

1. Crouch body, keep head upright.
2. Bounce ball by wrist action applied to ball with fingertips.

FOOTBALL SKILLS

477—Passing

1. Grasp ball with fingers spread; smaller hands grip ball more toward end of ball (lay ball on open hand, if necessary).
2. Hold ball at shoulder height, bringing ball behind ear during pass; keep elbow straight ahead and up.
3. Point opposite foot in direction of pass and release ball off fingertips.

478—Lateral Passing

1. Toss ball sideways or backwards with easy motion.
2. It does not have to spiral.
3. Shorter tosses are more effective.

479—Carrying Ball

1. Carry ball under outside arm.
2. Have one end of ball in palm of hand, other end of ball in armpit.

#477

#478

#479

480—Catching
1. Catch ball in hands, not against body.
2. Keep eyes on ball; give with it on contact.
3. Do not block vision with arms; keep little fingers or thumbs together on reception.

#480

#481

481—Blocking
1. Bend low and make contact with shoulder about waist high or above.
2. Blocker cannot leave feet in touch football.
3. Keep block on until ball carrier is past. Do not point in direction of block.

482—Centering
1. Spread feet shoulder width, knees bent.
2. The arms should extend slightly to grasp ball.
3. Right hand centers ball (held as for a pass); left hand guides ball (placed back slightly).

#482

#483

483—Stance (3-Point)
1. Feet are shoulder-width apart, toes pointed straight ahead.
2. Have toe of one foot even with heel of other.
3. Support hand is hand on side of extended foot.
4. Hand rests on knuckles.
5. Opposite hand rests on thigh.
6. Keep eyes forward at all times.

484—Kicking (Punting)

1. Feet are slightly spread, kicking foot about a foot to rear.
2. Catch ball in hands between shoulder and waist.
3. Step with kicking foot about one foot in front of other foot.
4. Then take natural step with other foot and bring kicking foot up (toes forward, contact on outside of instep).
5. Kicker should see foot meet ball. Have good follow-through.

#484

485—Hand-Offs

1. Hand-off with hand nearest ball carrier, elbow bent, ball about one foot from body (use both hands to start hand-off).
2. Ball is grasped by carrier with near arm chest high, palm down, elbow bent.
3. Far arm of receiver is waist high, palm up, elbow bent.

#485

VOLLEYBALL SKILLS

486—Service (Underhand)

1. Face opposite court with ball in left hand, keeping weight on right foot as right arm swings back to shoulder height.
2. Shift weight to left foot during forward swing, knocking ball out of left hand.
3. Follow through with whole body after ball is struck.

487—Receiving the Ball (Bump)

1. Have knees slightly flexed, keeping eyes on ball, and being alert for teammates' passes.
2. For a high ball, have hands up and take a small step forward, meeting ball with fingers relaxed.
3. For low ball, flex knees more and have fists together.

#487

Bump

488—Passing the Ball

1. Try to pass ball high in air for easier handling.
2. Direct it by turning hands.

489—Setup

1. This is a high (2 feet above net) easy pass which is about 1 foot from net.
2. Use a chest pass (push from the chest on a high ball) for the setup.

#489

SOCCER SKILLS

KICKING

491—Instep Kick

1. Swing leg straight forward, thigh extended backward and knee flexed.
2. Straighten knee and swing from hip to toe, keeping toe slightly flexed.
3. Follow through the kick.

492—Inside Foot Kick

1. Leg swings back with toe extended and knee slightly bent.
2. Leg swings forward, toe close to ground and turned outward, knee still bent.
3. Knee straightens upon contact which is when ball is in front of body.

493—Outside Foot Kick

Performed just as in kicking with inside foot, except contact is made with outside of foot.

494—Heel Kick

1. This is not recommended for beginners.
2. Step ahead of ball, propel it backwards with short snappy kick.

495—Kick for Distance

1. Kicking toe is up, and foot is at right angles with the line of the leg.
2. Get force in snap of the knee.
3. Keep opposite foot slightly behind ball.

#490

490—Spiking

1. This is a hard driving shot done by jumping high in the air, hitting the ball hard.
2. It must have good setup and is hard to return.

496—Trapping
1. This is stopping the ball and gaining possession of it as it approaches.
2. Easiest ways are:
   a. Trap slow balls with raised foot, toes up. Lower toes on contact to secure ball.
   b. Trap fast balls with leg. Set receiving foot at right angle to ball's flight. Upon contact bring opposite knee in to trap ball.

#496

497—Dribble
1. Tap ball alternately with insides of left and right feet.
2. Keep ball close to feet and under control.
3. Do not kick it and then run to catch up.

#497

498—Heading
1. Get under ball. Lower head slightly and stiffen neck.
2. Meet ball with upward and forward movement to control direction.
3. Keep eye on ball until impact.
4. This is difficult for younger children.

#498

499—Tackling
1. This is taking the ball away from another player with feet.
2. Steal ball from toes of opponent when it leaves his feet.

#499

500—Passing
1. Take weight on right foot, swing left leg back and forward.
2. Hit ball with inside of left foot.
3. Reverse procedure for forward left pass.
4. May also be done with toes, outside of foot, or head.

#500

TRACK AND FIELD SKILLS

STARTING POSITIONS

501—Standing Start
1. Place feet in comfortable position, one foot slightly back of other foot.
2. Runner leans forward slightly, takes off on rear foot at sound of "gun."

#502

502—Crouch Start (adapt to individual)
1. On your mark:
   a. Squat about one foot from starting line.
   b. Hands are placed back of line with weight on thumbs and fingers.
   c. Kneel on right knee, left foot even with right knee. Adjust width.
2. Get set:
   a. Rock forward and upward, hips down.
   b. Head up with weight on hands and front foot.
3. Go:
   a. Whip arms and push with front leg.
   b. Step forward on back leg and straighten up gradually.

503—Standing Broad Jump
1. Toe the line with both feet.
2. Crouch low, knees bent, arms back of hips.
3. Jump forward, carrying arms and feet forward and upward.
4. Land on both feet.

504—Running Broad Jump
1. Run 16-20 strides on approach. Take off one foot from approach.
2. Jump high in air, tuck body as if in a chair, and bring feet together.
3. Land with legs forward and arms back. Thrust arms forward upon landing to get forward body fall.

505—Scissors Jump (High Jump)

1. Approach from either left or right (choice of jumper).
2. Stand at 45° angle to bar. Run to gain momentum.
3. Number of steps depends on runner (7, 9, 11, etc.).
4. Runner approaching right side takes off with left foot, swinging right foot over bar. Left leg follows like scissors. Keep legs straight.
5. The landing is made on the lead foot followed by the rear foot.

#505

#506

506—Western Roll (High Jump)

1. Approach from left and in the scissors jump. Have left shoulder toward bar at takeoff.
2. Take off on left foot, swinging the right leg forward and over. Left leg tucks at the side of the right and the jumper rolls over the bar.
3. Land on left foot and hands.

507—Passing Baton

1. Must be passed in a 20-yard interval.
2. Runner carries baton in left hand. Receiver grabs it palm up on open right hand.
3. Receiver starts to run when runner is 5-7 yards behind, timing speed to exchange baton at full speed.

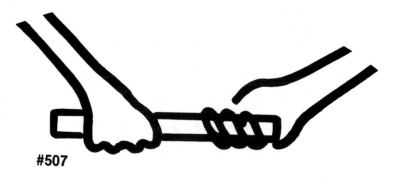

#507

Lead-Up Games for Team Sports

508—Throw It and Run Softball

Softball, three bases

1. Have two teams with 7-11 on each side.
2. The game is played like regular softball except the batting is eliminated.
3. One player for the fielders throws the ball to the catcher. The thrower must catch the ball and throw it out into the field. The fielders then must retrieve the ball and return it to the catcher before the thrower runs to first base and back.
   a. The thrower does not have to catch bad balls (4 of these constitute a run).
   b. Three misses and thrower is out. A caught fly is also an out. Foul balls are strikes.
   c. Three outs and teams change.

509—Touchdown

Small object for "ball"

1. Game begins with one team going into a huddle on their goal line to decide which player will carry the object (eraser, chalk, marble).
2. Then the team runs to the other goal line, each pretending to have the object.
3. The other team tries to tag the player they think has the object (any player tagged must stop immediately and show hands).
4. If the player with the object gets through safely, he yells, "Touchdown," and a point is scored.
5. If a team scores a point, they keep the object for another try. If not, the other team gets it.

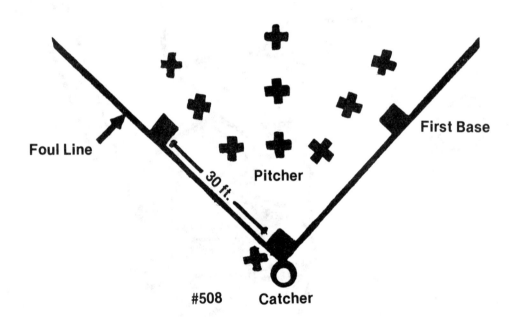

Foul Line

30 ft.

Pitcher

First Base

#508　Catcher

510—Triple Charge

1. Players form a large circle, and count off in threes.
2. Three players, numbered one, two, and three, are in the center.
3. Each center player takes a turn calling out his number. All those with that number exchange places.
4. The center player tries to find an empty place.
5. The player without a place then goes into the center.

#510

511—Two Square

Volleyball or playground ball

1. Two squares are drawn off as at right.
2. Player #1 begins by serving ball from behind base line. Ball may be served and played on first bounce only.
3. Ball can only be struck underhand.
4. If foul or miss occurs, that player is eliminated.
5. Fouls:
   a. Hitting ball in any manner other than underhand
   b. Ball landing out of bounds or on center line
   c. Handling ball in any manner other than striking it underhand

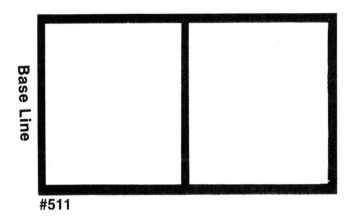

#511

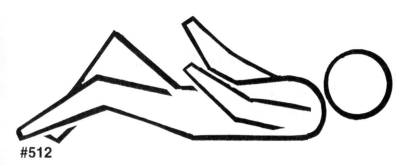

#512

513—Twenty-One

Basketball

1. Players form in file by one basket of basketball court.
2. Each player takes a turn shooting a long shot from the free-throw line and a short shot from where ball is received.
3. A ball that goes out of bounds is shot from where it goes out.
4. Long shot counts two, short shot counts one.
5. First player to score twenty-one points wins.

512—Turtle Tag

1. One child is "it" and chases the others to tag one of them.
2. Children avoid being tagged by lying on their backs as turtles.
3. If tagged when not on his back, that person is "it."

#513

514—Two Deep

1. Players form circle at about double arm's length apart.
2. A runner and chaser are chosen to begin. The chaser tries to tag the runner.
3. To avoid being tagged, the runner stops in front of a player in the circle. This player then becomes the runner.
4. If tagged, runner and chaser exchange.
5. Changes should be frequent.

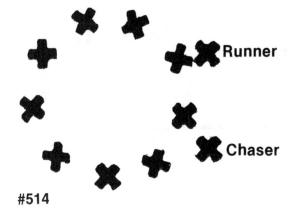

Runner

Chaser

#514

127

515—Wall Volley

Volleyball

1. Player stands behind a line five feet from a wall and about five feet long.
2. He is given an allotted time (15-30 seconds) to bounce ball against wall as many times as possible.
3. Ball should be volleyed above a line on the wall about six feet high.
4. If he misses, he does not finish the time period given.
5. Can be played with teams or on an individual basis.

517—Two-Pitch Softball

Softball, bat

Regular softball rules, except:

a. Member of team at bat is the pitcher (for better pitching).
b. Batter gets only two pitches to hit **fair** ball (regardless of type of pitch) or he is **out.**

516—Volleyball

Volleyball, net

1. Game begins with the right back serving the ball from serving area. Ball must travel over the net on first serve.
2. If opponents fail to return it, a point is made (only serving team can score).
3. If serving team fails to return ball successfully, "side out" is declared, and the serve changes teams.
4. Server continues until "side out" is declared.
5. Team rotates clockwise each time they receive the serve.
6. Ball may be hit three times by a team before returning it. A player may not touch it twice in succession.
7. A "double foul" results in a replay of that point.
8. Variations may be made according to age.
9. Rules:

a. Players may not touch net or cross center line.
b. Ball is in play on boundary lines.
c. Net is seven feet high for junior-high level (height of extended arm).
d. Ball must be batted or volleyed, not held or carried.
e. Game is 15 points.

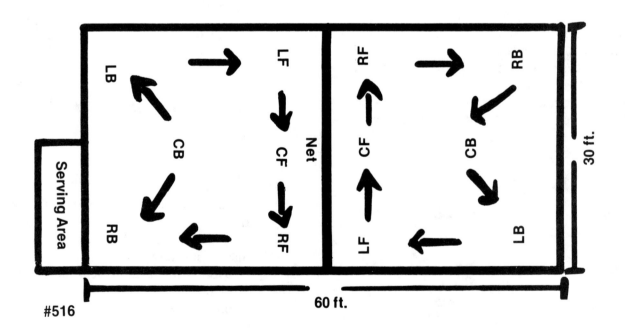

#516

60 ft.

30 ft.

Physical Fitness Tests

September 1980

President's Council on Physical Fitness and Sports

For sale by the Superintendent of Documents, U.S. Government Printing Office
Washington, D.C. 20402

518—Standing Broad Jump

1. Allow three trials.
2. Measure from the takeoff line to the heel or any part of body that touches the surface nearest the takeoff line.
3. Record best of three trials in feet and inches to the nearest inch.

#518

519—600-Yard Run—Walk

1. Walking is permitted, but the object is to cover the distance in the shortest possible time.
2. Record the time in minutes and seconds.

NOTE— It is possible to test several pupils at the same time. Have the pupils pair off before the start of the test. One of the partners runs, while the other stands near the timer. The timer calls out the time continuously, until the runners have all crossed the finish line. Each pupil near the timer listens for, and remembers, his partner's time as the latter finishes.

520—Softball Throw for Distance

1. Only an overhand throw may be used.
2. Mark point where ball lands with one of the stakes.
3. Three throws are allowed.
4. Disqualify throw if pupil steps over restraining line.

#520

521—Grass Drills

Grass drills are strenuous. They are performed in quick succession and at top speed. Consequently, they are continued for short periods of time. These drills should be preceded with general warm-up activities and fundamental exercises. Progression is gained by gradually increasing the length of time devoted to the grass drills as physical condition improves. The grass drills are executed in place. Insist on top speed performance.

Grass drills involve moving rapidly from one to the other of three basic positions:

1. **Go**—running in place at top speed on the toes and balls of the feet, knees raised high, arms pumping, body bent slightly forward at the waist.
2. **Front**—prone position, palms flat on the ground directly under the shoulders, legs together and extended.
3. **Back**—supine position (flat on the back), arms extended alongside the body with palms down, legs together and straight.

The drill is conducted by giving the commands, "Go," "Front," "Back," changing the sequence continuously. Allow sufficient time between commands for pupils to assume proper position.

522—Shuttle Run

Equipment: Two blocks of wood, 2" x 2" x 4" (chalkboard erasers may be used), stopwatch. Mark two parallel lines 30 feet apart. Place the blocks of wood behind one of the lines.

Starting Position: Pupil stands behind the line opposite the blocks, ready to run.

Action: On the signal, "Ready! Go!" the pupil runs to the blocks, picks up one, returns and places it behind the starting line. (He does not throw or drop it.) He then runs and picks up the **second block** and carries **it back across** the starting line.

1. Allow two trials.
2. **Disqualify** any trial in which the block **is dropped** or thrown.
3. Record the better of the two trials in seconds to the nearest tenth.

30 ft.

#522

523—Fifty-Yard Dash

1. The score is the lapsed time between the starter's signal and the instant the pupil crosses the finish line.
2. Record the time in seconds to the nearest tenth.

524—Sit-Ups

1. Sit up and turn the trunk to the left. Touch the right elbow to the left knee.
2. Return to starting position.
3. Sit up and turn the trunk to the right, touching the left elbow to the right knee.

#524

525—Pull-Ups (Boys)

Equipment: A bar of sufficient height and comfortable to grip.

Starting Position: Grasp the bar with palms facing forward; hang with arms and legs fully extended. Feet must be free of floor. The partner stands slightly to one side of the pupil being tested and counts each successful pull-up.

Action:

1. Pull body up with the arms until the chin is placed over the bar.
2. Lower body until the elbows are fully extended.
3. Repeat the exercise as many times as possible.

#525

526—Flexed-Arm Hang (Girls)

Equipment: A stopwatch and a sturdy bar, comfortable to grip and adjustable in height (height of bar should be approximately the same as the pupil being tested).

Starting Position: Using an overhand grip, the pupil hangs with chin above bar and elbows flexed. Legs must be straight and feet free of floor.

Action:

1. Hold position as long as possible.
2. Timing should start as soon as pupil is in position and released from any support other than her own.
3. Timing should stop when the pupil's chin touches or drops below the bar.
4. Knees must not be raised and kicking is not permitted.

#526

The standards listed below must be achieved by boys and girls to qualify for the Presidential Physical Fitness Award. These are actual 85th percentile scores on the test items and are not arbitrary standards.

BOYS

Age	Sit-Ups (flexed leg)	Pull-Ups	Standing Broad Jump	50-Yard Dash	600-Yard Run—Walk	Ages 10-12 1-Mile or 9-Min. Run*		Ages 13 and over 1½-Mile or 12-Min. Run*		Shuttle Run
	1 min.					Time	Yards	Time	Yards	
10	42	5	5'8''	:7.7	2:11	7:06	2081			:10.4
11	43	5	5'10''	:7.4	2:09	6:43	2143			:10.1
12	45	6	6'1''	:7.1	2:00	6:20	2205			:10.0
13	48	7	6'8''	:6.9	1:54			9:40	3037	:09.7
14	50	9	6'11''	:6.5	1:47			9:40	3037	:09.3
15	50	11	7'5''	:6.3	1:42			9:40	3037	:09.2
16	50	11	7'9''	:6.3	1:40			9:40	3037	:09.1
17	49	12	8'0''	:6.1	1:38			9:40	3037	:09.0

*Options. For 600-Yard Run—Walk

GIRLS

Age	Sit-Ups (flexed leg)	Flexed-Arm Hang	Standing Broad Jump	50-Yard Dash	600-Yard Run—Walk	Ages 10-12 1-Mile or 9-Min. Run*		Ages 13 and over 1½-Mile or 12-Min. Run*		Shuttle Run
	1 min.					Time	Yards	Time	Yards	
10	38	:24	5'5''	:7.8	2:30	8:33	1801			:10.9
11	38	:24	5'7''	:7.5	2:25	8:02	1824			:10.5
12	38	:23	5'9''	:7.4	2:21	7:28	1847			:10.5
13	40	:21	6'0''	:7.2	2:16			14:00	2232	:10.2
14	41	:26	6'3''	:7.1	2:11			14:00	2232	:10.1
15	40	:25	6'1''	:7.1	2:14			14:00	2232	:10.2
16	38	:20	6'0''	:7.3	2:19			14:00	2232	:10.4
17	40	:22	6'3''	:7.1	2:14			14:00	2232	:10.1

*Options. For 600-Yard Run—Walk

THE TEST

Already widely used throughout the country, the AAHPER Youth Fitness Test assesses physical strength, stamina, speed, agility, and coordination. The test items are sit-ups, shuttle run, standing broad jump, 50-yard dash, softball throw, 600-yard run, and pull-ups for boys and the flexed-arm hang for girls.

First Aid in the Classroom

FIRST Things FIRST!

1. Keep **CALM!**

2. **IMMEDIATE ATTENTION:**

   a. **Open airway**—start mouth-to-mouth resuscitation if breathing has stopped and CPR if circulation has stopped
   b. **Stop the bleeding.**
   c. **Treat for shock** (see fainting).
   d. **Wash chemicals away** (eyes, skin, or mucous membranes) with water—lots of water— continuous water up to 20 minutes if necessary.

3. If immediate medical attention is needed, contact physician first; otherwise, contact parents first.

BREATHING

When child is not breathing, lay him/her flat on back, tilt head back and hold jaw firmly in jutting position (so tongue won't fall back and close airway). Start mouth-to-mouth breathing, with mouth over child's nose and mouth.

CIRCULATION

CARDIOPULMONARY RESUSCITATION (CPR)—Teachers are encouraged to become certified in CPR.

When circulation and breathing stops, give rhythmic pressure over the lower portion of sternum (breastbone)—ratio 15 compressions, then 2 breaths (mouth-to-mouth). If two rescuers are working, give one breath for every 5 compressions.

CUTS, SCRAPES, SCRATCHES

Small, superficial abrasions and cuts require control of bleeding (direct pressure over wound with sterile gauze pad or handkerchief). Cleanse with soap and water and cover with sterile gauze.

BLEEDING

All Bleeding: Direct pressure over wound. Use sterile gauze pad, handkerchief or hand.

Deep Wounds: Those requiring stitching or involving bone need medical attention promptly. Don't try to wash deep wounds. Control bleeding and contact physician.

Puncture Wounds: Tetanus may be involved. Advise parents to contact physician.

Nose Bleeds: Press or pinch sides of nose tightly against midline partition for several minutes. Have child sit up. Discourage nose blowing.

Pulsating Bleeding: Arterial bleeding is often profuse. Apply firm pressure on heart side of wound or over wound itself. "Pressure point" compression may be needed. These "pressure points" are in the groin area and midway up the inner aspect of upper arms.

Tourniquets are not recommended. However, if it is necessary to apply one, contact physician immediately. Be certain physician knows tourniquet is on and when it was applied.

SPINAL INJURIES

If there are severe injuries, if child complains of pain in back, or if a deformity is noted, suspect a fracture or dislocation. Don't move child. Don't try to move bones to straighten them. Keep child warm and quiet. Treat shock or bleeding if indicated.

SHOCK

Due to trauma, hemorrhage, fracture, or burn—child is pale, cold, sweating and has rapid and weak pulse. Keep warm (blanket underneath child if possible). Keep horizontal with head flat (remember, don't move head or neck if spinal injuries are suspected). Give nothing by mouth. Contact physician immediately.

BURNS

Chemical: Wash area with water for several minutes. Contact parents.

Heat Burns: 1st and 2nd degree—skin reddened and blistered.

Apply water by immersion or soaking cloths, until pain does not recur when water is removed.

3rd degree—whole skin destroyed (or extensive 2nd degree).

Treat for shock.

Remove clothing, rings, etc., if possible.

Cover with sterile dressings, clean sheet or towel around, over, but not on the burned area.

Do not apply anything to burn. Do not give anything by mouth.

Contact physician immediately.

HEAD INJURIES

Treat all head injuries like a neck injury.

If possible, have child lie down with head slightly elevated.

Contact parents.

Contact physician if: Deformity, swelling, loss of consciousness, vomiting, change in breathing, size of pupils of eyes different, bleeding from scalp, nose, ears.

FAINTING

Usually due to excitement or anxiety.

Calm waiting. Loosen clothing. Allow child to lie down until recovered (see shock).

SEIZURE AND CONVULSIONS

Be calm. Gently ease child down, remove furniture, etc., to prevent injuries. Loosen clothing. If aspiration is suspected, child may be placed on his/her side.

Wait for seizure to subside. **Your** actions will help witnesses to adjust properly.

Encourage child to rest and sleep. Teacher should know who is subject to seizures. If child's first seizure, call parents.

TEETH

Broken tooth—contact parents.
Whole tooth knocked out—**reinsert whole tooth if possible** or save and give to parents to take to dentist.

INSECT STINGS

Scrape out stinger with fingernail (don't pull it out)—cold compresses.

Contact physician if reactions occur: hives, rash, pallor, weakness, thick tongue or lips, tingling of tongue or lips, nausea, vomiting, "tightness" in chest, nose or throat, or collapse.

Start mouth-to-mouth resuscitation and/or CPR if indicated.

ABDOMINAL PAIN

Mild pain usually responds to rest and time. If prolonged, contact parents.

Severe pain accompanied by vomiting, fever, bloody stools, or due to blow to abdomen, notify parents.

DOG BITES

Wash wound with soap and water immediately.

Identify the animal.

Contact parents.

Notify Health Department.

SNAKEBITES

Nonpoisonous: Treat as cut, contact parents.

Poisonous: Keep child quiet, contact physician, contact parents.

If snakebite kit available, follow directions.

Identify snake.

FRACTURES

If skin is opened, cover with sterile dressing.
Never push, pull, or manipulate protruding bone.

FROSTBITE

Don't rub, squeeze, or manipulate.

Treat injured part with extreme gentleness.

Don't apply snow or cold water.

Applying clothing to prevent further injury is indicated.

Contact parents.

SUSPECTED COMMUNICABLE DISEASES—SEND HOME!

When **two or more** of any of the following symptoms are present, a communicable disease may be suspected: headache, red eyes, running nose, cough, fever, rash, sore throat, vomiting, diarrhea.

1. Separate from other children.
2. Contact parents to arrange transportation.
3. Observe child.
4. Water may be given.
5. Make child as comfortable as possible.

POISON

Poisoning by mouth: hurry is the word to associate with poisoning by mouth. Objectives: to dilute the poison as fast as possible, then, except as advised, to induce vomiting.

WHEN YOU DO NOT KNOW WHAT POISON the victim has swallowed:

1. Dilute the poison with water or milk.
2. Try to find out what poison has been swallowed (look for the original container).
3. **Get medical help** immediately.

WHEN YOU KNOW THAT THE VICTIM HAS NOT SWALLOWED A STRONG ACID, STRONG ALKALI, OR PETROLEUM PRODUCT, but you do not have the original container:

1. **Dilute the poison** with water or milk.
2. **Induce vomiting** (except for strong acids, strong alkalis, and petroleum products).
3. **Get medical help** immediately.

FIRST AID ROOM AND SUPPLIES

cot	soap
blanket and sheets	tweezers
sterile cotton balls	snakebite kit (optional)
splints	scissors
3" x 3" muslin squares	sterile gauze roller bandages
adhesive tape	Band-Aids
sterile gauze pads	safety pins

Equipment You Can Make

Balance Beams can easily be made with any height desired from lumber.

Rocker Boards can also be made from required lumber. 1'' x 6'' x 3'' with edging, 2'' to 5'' roller.

Pinnies can easily be made from scrap material.

Inner Tubes: Bicycle or tractor tire inner tubes (all different sizes) can be used for resistive or creative exercising.

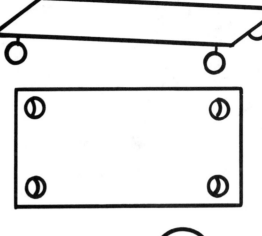

Scooter Boards: Use ¾'' plywood, cut in 12'' x 12'' pieces, and attach four casters with rubber wheels to each corner.

Batting Tees can be made from traffic cones or simply with plastic tubing in a board.

Frisbees: Plastic lids as they are can be used for frisbees. With the center cut out, the plastic lids can be used for ring-toss games.

Lummi Sticks: Broomsticks can be used for lummi sticks.

Streamers: Crepe paper strips can be used for streamers for rhythm and movement exploration.

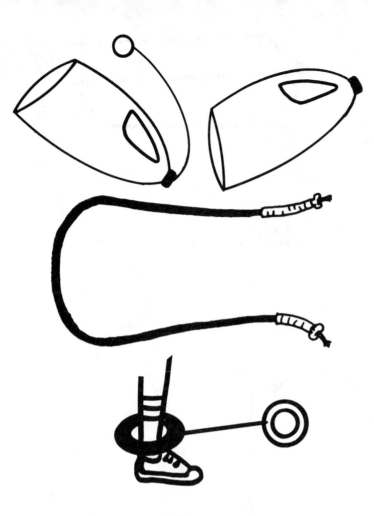

Scoopers or Catchers: Bottles can also be used for scoopers or catchers. Make a hole in the plastic bottle; then cut at an angle for the scoop effect.

Handles for Jump Ropes: Garden hose can be used for handles for jump ropes.

Ring Toss and Ankle Hop: With a small wooden peg (dowel), attach both ends of the hose so they cover the peg. Next staple the hose to the peg. Tape all sharp edges. These rings can be used for ring toss or rings of different lengths can be used for ankle hop games.

Golf Holes: Tin cans can be used for golf holes. The cans can be set in a premade hole with dirt surrounding the can tightly.

Stilts: Modified stilts can be made out of coffee cans and long strings. Again, all sharp edges are to be taped.

Rackets for Yarn Balls and Paper Balls: Bend hanger from original position to square, slip a nylon stocking over square hanger and bend hook back to make handle. Cover loose and sharp edges with tape.

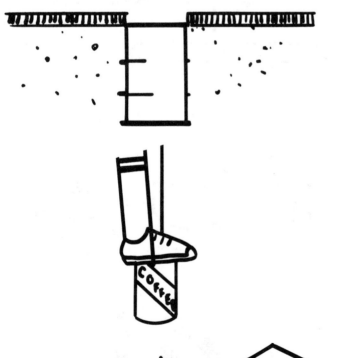

Field Marker: Bottle used as a field marker or marker of any kind. Add a flag and fill the bottom with sand or dirt for stability.

Bowling Pins: Milk cartons can be used for bowling pins with the ball made from yarn, paper covered with tape, stocking ball, or sponge.

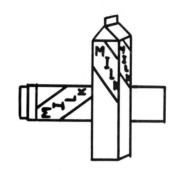

Old Tires set into the ground can be used for playground articles to sit on, crawl under, and play on.

Gym Floor Skates: Two pieces of carpet (12'' x 12'') with carpet side on the gym floor and the rubber mat facing the ceiling can be used for gym floor skates. Sit on carpet (16'' x 16'') and push with feet or kneel on carpet and push a partner.

Elastic Ropes or Cord purchased in department store can be used for exercise and creativity in movement.

Target Boards can be made simply by cutting plywood and painting the target on the board.

Beanbags: Use remnant material (old school uniforms or jerseys) and cut two 5" x 5" squares. Put right sides of material together and sew three of the four sides. Turn inside out and fill pouch with tiny pebbles or beans. Now hand stitch or sew the fourth side together, tucking in the edges.

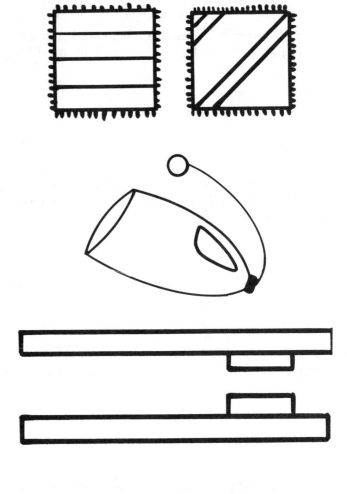

A Toss and Catch Toy can also be made with a scoop-cut bottle. Add string with ball attached.

Stilts: Begin with an 8' 2 x 4. Cut off one foot and divide in half for feet pieces. Cut the rest of board in two, and nail on the 6" boards at the ends of the 3½' boards.

High Jump Standards: The wooden poles have pegs 6" apart, ranging from a 6" mark to a 6' mark consecutively. The poles are based by two crossing boards. The pole can be easily manipulated to any desired length.

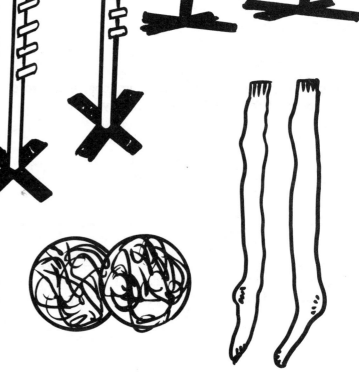

Hurdles: The hurdles are made the same as the high jump standards but smaller and fewer pegs.

Balls can easily be made from yarn, paper covered with tape, sponge, or by stuffing nylons in the toe of a sock and sewing closed (stocking ball).